SOLUTIONS MANUAL TO ACCOMPANY

Second Edition

Nonlinear Programming

Theory and Algorithms

Mokhtar S. Bazaraa
American Airlines Decision Technologies
Dallas, Texas

Hanif D. Sherali
Department of Industrial and Systems Engineering
Virginia Polytechnic Institute and State University
Blacksburg, Virginia

C. M. Shetty
School of Industrial and Systems Engineering
Georgia Institute of Technology
Atlanta, Georgia

Prepared by

Joanna M. Leleno

John Wiley & Sons, Inc.
New York • Chichester • Brisbane • Toronto • Singapore

TABLE OF CONTENTS

Chapter 1

    1.1, 1.2, 1.7, 1.11, 1.12, 1.14

Chapter 2

    2.3, 2.6, 2.9, 2.11, 2.14, 2.17, 2.18, 2.19, 2.21, 2.22, 2.23, 2.26, 2.35, 2.46, 2.55

Chapter 3

    3.3, 3.5, 3.7, 3.12, 3.13, 3.17, 3.20, 3.24, 3.26, 3.30, 3.35, 3.42, 3.43, 3.44, 3.47, 3.52, 3.57, 3.58, 3.59, 3.60, 3.65, 3.66

Chapter 4

    4.1, 4.4, 4.6, 4.8, 4.10, 4.15, 4.17, 4.18, 4.19, 4.23, 4.24, 4.25, 4.26, 4.27, 4.28, 4.29, 4.31

Chapter 5

    5.3, 5.6, 5.7, 5.10, 5.15

Chapter 6

    6.2, 6.4, 6.7, 6.10, 6.15, 6.17, 6.18, 6.28

Chapter 7

    7.5, 7.6, 7.7, 7.8, 7.11, 7.17

Chapter 8

    8.4, 8.15, 8.18, 8.19, 8.20, 8.33, 8.55

Chapter 9

    9.3, 9.5, 9.11, 9.12, 9.16, 9.17, 9.18, 9.30

Chapter 10

    10.3, 10.12, 10.17, 10.19, 10.30, 10.37, 10.42, 10.43, 10.50

Chapter 11

    11.3, 11.5, 11.14, 11.20, 11.22, 11.23, 11.31, 11.34, 11.37, 11.41, 11.42, 11.43

ANSWERS TO SELECTED EXERCISES

IN CHAPTER 1

1.1. In figure below, x_{min} and x_{max} denote optimal solutions for part (a) and part (b), respectively.

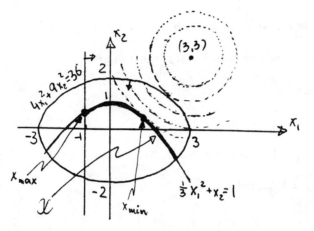

1.2. Let X denote the set of feasible portfolios. The task is to find an $x^* \in X$ such that

for any $x \in X$ if $c^t x \geq c^t x^*$ then $x^t V x > x^{*t} V x^*$.

One way to find efficient portfolios is to solve a problem in which the expected return is maximized on X, and another one in which the variance is minimized on X. If $\overline{x}$ is a unique expected-return-maximizer, then it readily is an efficient portfolio. If alternative solutions exist, then one with the smallest variance is an efficient portfolio. Similar procedure can be applied to the set of optimal solutions to the variance minimization problem.

1.7. We need to find a positive number K that minimizes the expected total cost. The expected total cost is $\alpha(1-p)P(\overline{x} \leq K|\mu_2) + \beta p P(\overline{x} > K|\mu_1)$. Therefore, the mathematical programming problem can be formulated as

$$\text{Minimize} \quad \alpha(1-p)\int_0^K f(\overline{x}|\mu_2)d\overline{x} + \beta p \int_K^\infty f(\overline{x}|\mu_1)dx$$
$$\text{subject to } K \geq 0.$$

If conditional distribution functions $F(x|\mu_2)$ and $F(x|\mu_1)$ are known, then the objective function is simply $\alpha(1-p)F(K|\mu_2) + \beta p(1-F(K|\mu_1))$.

1.11. Let x and p denote demand and production level, respectively. Z denotes a standard normal random variable. Then we need p to be such that $P(p < x - 5) \leq 0.01$, which by continuity of the normal random variable is equivalent to $P(x \geq p + 5) \leq 0.01$. Therefore, p must satisfy

$$P(Z \geq \frac{p-95}{6}) \leq 0.01,$$

where Z is a standard normal random variable. From tables of the standard normal distribution we have $P(Z \geq -1.282) = 0.01$. Therefore, the chance constraint is equivalent to $p \geq 87.308$.

1.12. Notation: x_j - production in period j, $j = 1, ..., n$

d_j - demand in period j, $j = 1, ..., n$

I_j - inventory at the end of period j, $j = 0, 1, ,,,, n$.

minimize $\sum\limits_{j=1}^{n} [f(x_j) + cI_{j-1}]$

subject to

$x_j - d_j + I_{j-1} = I_j$ for $j = 1, ..., n$

$I_j \leq K$ for $j = 1, ..., n\text{-}1$

$I_n = 0$

$x_j \geq 0$, $I_j \geq 0$ for $j = 1, ..., n$.

1.14. a. The total cost per time unit (day) is to be minimized given the storage limitations.

minimize $f(Q_1, Q_2) = k_1\frac{d_1}{Q_1} + h_1\frac{Q_1}{2} + k_2\frac{d_2}{Q_2} + h_2\frac{Q_2}{2} + c_1d_1 + c_2d_2$

subject to $s_1Q_1 + s_2Q_2 \leq S$

$Q_1 > 0, Q_2 > 0$.

Note that the last two terms in the objective function are constant and thus can be ignored while solving this problem.

b. Let S_j denote lost sales (in each cycle) of product j, $j = 1, 2$. In this case replace the objective function in part (a) with $F(Q_1, Q_2, S_1, S_2)$, where $F(Q_1, Q_2, S_1, S_2) = F_1(Q_1, S_1) + F_2(Q_2, S_2)$, and where

$$F_j(Q_j, S_j) = \frac{d_j}{Q_j + S_j} (k_j + c_jQ_j + l_jS_j - PQ_j) + h_j\frac{Q_j^2}{2(Q_j + S_j)} , j = 1, 2.$$

ANSWERS TO SELECTED EXERCISES

IN CHAPTER 2

2.3. $S_1 + S_2 = \{ (x_1, x_2) : 0 \leq x_1 \leq 1, \ 2 \leq x_2 \leq 3\}$

$S_1 - S_2 = \{ (x_1, x_2) : -1 \leq x_1 \leq 0, \ -2 \leq x_2 \leq -1\}$

2.6. Let $x \in H(S_1 \cap S_2)$. Then there exists $\lambda \in [0, 1]$ and $x_1, x_2 \in S_1 \cap S_2$ such that $x = \lambda x_1 + (1-\lambda)x_2$. Since x_1 and x_2 are both in S_1, and S_1 is a convex set, x must be S_1, and hence in $H(S_1)$. By similar arguments, x must be in $H(S_2)$. Therefore, $x \in H(S_1) \cap H(S_2)$.

Example in which $H(S_1 \cap S_2) \neq H(S_1) \cap H(S_2)$:

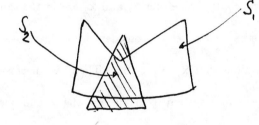

2.9. Let $S = S_1 + S_2$. Consider any $y, z \in S$, and any $\lambda \in (0, 1)$. Then there exist vectors $x_1, u_1 \in S_1$, and $x_2, u_2 \in S_2$, such that $\lambda y + (1-\lambda)z = \lambda x_1 + \lambda x_2 + (1-\lambda)u_1 + (1-\lambda)u_2$. Since both sets S_1 and S_2 are convex, we have $\lambda x_i + (1-\lambda)u_i \in S_i$, i = 1, 2. Therefore, $\lambda y + (1-\lambda)z$ is still a sum of a vector from S_1 and a vector from S_2, hence it is in S. Thus S is a convex set.

Next we show that if S_1 is compact, and S_2 is closed, then S is closed. Consider a convergent sequence $\{z_n\}$ of points from S, and let z denote its limit. By definition, $z_n = x_n + u_n$, where for each n, $x_n \in S_1$, and $u_n \in S_2$. Since $\{x_n\}$ is a sequence of points from a compact set, it must be bounded, and hence it has a convergent subsequence. For notational simplicity and without loss of generality, assume that the sequence $\{x_n\}$ itself is convergent, and let x denote its limit. Readily, $x \in S_1$. This result taken together with the convergence of the sequence $\{z_n\}$ implies that

$\{y_n\}$ is convergent. The limit, y, of $\{y_n\}$ must be in S_2, since S_2 is a closed set. Thus, z = x + y, where $x \in S_1$, $y \in S_2$, and therefore, $z \in S$. This completes the proof. □

2.11. For the existence and uniqueness proof see for example *Linear Algebra and Its Applications* by Gilbert Strang (Harcourt Brace Jovanovich, Inc., 1988).

If L = $\{ (x_1, x_2, x_3): 2x_1+x_2-x_3 + 0\}$, then L is the nullspace of A = [2 1 −1], and its orthogonal complement is the row space of A. Therefore, x_1 and x_2 are orthogonal projections of x onto L, and $L^{\perp}$, respectively. If x = (1 2 3), then $x_1 = \frac{1}{6}(14 \quad 11 \quad 19)$ and $x_2 = \frac{1}{6}(2 \quad 1 \quad -1)$.

2.14. a. First we show that $H(S) \subseteq \overline{S}$. For this purpose let us consider a vector $x \in H(S)$. By the definition of a convex hull, x must be a convex combination of some two points from S. That is there exist vectors x_1 and x_2, both in S, such that $x = \alpha x_1+(1-\alpha)x_2$ for some $\alpha \in [0,1]$. Furthermore, using the definition of S, we conclude that either x_1 and x_2 are in the same set (S_1 or S_2) or they must be elements of two distinct sets. Let us consider the former case first. For simplicity and without loss of generality assume that $x_1, x_2 \in S_1$. Then we necessarily have $A_1x_1 \leq b_1$ and $A_1x_2 \leq b_1$. By multiplying the first system by $\alpha \geq 0$, and the second one by $1-\alpha \geq 0$, we obtain $A_1x \leq b_1$. Thus $x \in \overline{S}$ (take $\lambda_1=1$, and $\lambda_2 = 0$ in the definition of the set $\overline{S}$).

Next, let us consider the case in which x_1 and x_2 are not elements of the same set S_i. Again, for simplicity and without loss of generality, assume that $x_1 \in S_1$ and $x_2 \in S_2$. Then $A_1x_1 \leq b_1$ and $A_2x_2 \leq b_2$. Let us select any number $\lambda \in (0, 1)$, and divide the first system by λ and the second system by $1-\lambda$. The outcome of these operations can be rewritten as $A_1y \leq \lambda_1b_1$, $A_2z \leq \lambda_2b_2$, where $\lambda_1 = \lambda$, $\lambda_2 = 1-\lambda_1$, $y = \frac{1}{\lambda_1}x_1$ and $z = \frac{1}{\lambda_2}x_2$. Again, by implementing the definition of $\overline{S}$, we conclude that $x \in \overline{S}$.

In the second part of the proof we need to show that $\overline{S} \subseteq H(S)$. Let $x \in \overline{S}$. Then, there exist vectors y and z such that x = y+z, and $A_1y \leq b_1\lambda_1$, $A_2z \leq b_2\lambda_2$ for some $\lambda_1, \lambda_2 \geq 0$, and such that $\lambda_1+\lambda_2=1$. If $\lambda_1=0$ or $\lambda_2 = 0$, then we readily obtain $x \in S$, thus $x \in H(S)$. If $\lambda_1>0$ and $\lambda_2>0$, then

$x = \lambda_1 y_1 + \lambda_2 z_2$, where $y_1 = \frac{1}{\lambda_1} y$ and $z_2 = \frac{1}{\lambda_2} z$. It can be easily verified that in this case $y_1 \in S_1$ and $z_2 \in S_2$, which implies that both vectors y_1 and z_2 are in S. Therefore, x is a convex combination of points in S, hence $x \in H(S)$. This completes the proof. $\square$

b. Set S is a union of two polytopes, hence H(S) is the set of all convex combinations of vertices of S_1 and S_2, hence H(S) is closed. Therefore, cl H(S) = H(S), which together with part (a) gives cl H(S) = $\overline{S}$. $\square$

2.17. Consider the system $A^t y = c$, $y \geq 0$:

$$y_1 \ + 2y_2 = 1$$
$$-y_1 + 2y_2 = 0$$
$$-y_1 \qquad = 5$$
$$y_1 \geq 0, \ y_2 \geq 0.$$

The first two equations yield $y_1 = 1/2$, while the third equation gives $y_1 = -5$. Therefore, this system has no solution. By Farkas' Theorem we then conclude that the system $Ax \leq 0$, $c^t x > 0$ has a solution.

2.18. ($\Rightarrow$) We show that if System 2 has a solution, then System 1 is inconsistent. Suppose that System 2 is consistent and let y_0 be its solution. If System 1 has a solution, x_0, say, then we necessarily have $x_0^t A y = 0$. However, since $x_0^t A = c^t$, this result leads to $c^t y_0 = 0$, thus contradicting $c^t y_0 = 1$. Therefore, System 1 must be inconsistent.

($\Leftarrow$) In this part we show that if System 2 has no solution, then System 1 has one. Assume that System 2 has no solution, and let $S = \{(z_1, z_0) : z_1 = -A^t y, z_0 = c^t y, y \in E_m\}$. S is a nonempty convex set, and $(z, z_0) = (0, 1) \notin S$. Therefore, there exists a nonzero vector (p_1, p_0) and a real number α such that $p_1^t z_1 + p_0 z_0 \leq \alpha < p^t 0 + p_0$ for any $(z, z_0) \in S$. By the definition of S, this implies that $-p_1^t A^t y + p_0 c^t y \leq \alpha < p_0$ for any $y \in E_m$. In particular for $y = 0$, we obtain $0 \leq \alpha < p_0$. Next, let us remark that since α is nonnegative and $(-p_1^t A^t + p_0 c^t)y \leq \alpha$ for any $y \in E_m$, then we necessarily have $-p^t A^t + p_0 c^t = 0$ (or else y can be made sufficiently large to violate this inequality). We have thus shown that there exists a vector (p_1, p_0) where $p_0 > 0$, such that $Ap_1 - p_0c = 0$. By letting $x = \frac{1}{p_0}p_1$, we conclude that x solves the system $Ax - c = 0$. This shows that System 1 has a solution. $\qquad \Box$

2.19. ($\Rightarrow$) We show that if System 1 has a solution, $\overline{x}$, then System 2 is inconsistent. By contradiction, suppose that System 2 has a solution $\overline{y}$. Then $A\overline{x} = c$ and $A^t\overline{y} = 0$, $c^t\overline{y} = 1$. Therefore, $\overline{y}^tA\overline{x} = c^t\overline{y} = 1$. However, $\overline{y}^tA = 0$, hence a contradiction results. Therefore, if System 1 has a solution, then System 2 is inconsistent.

($\Leftarrow$) We prove that if System 1 has no solution, then System 2 has one. If System 1 has no solution, then vector c is not in the column space of matrix A. Furthermore, from linear algebra, we conclude that vector c is not orthogonal to all vectors in the nullspace of A^t (orthogonal complement of the column space of A). That is, there exists $\hat{y}$ such that $A^t\hat{y} = 0$ and $c^t\hat{y} \neq 0$. It can be easily verified that $\overline{y} = \frac{1}{c^t\hat{y}}\hat{y}$ solves System 2. This completes the proof. $\qquad \Box$

2.21. See the answer to Exercise 2.22.

2.22. ($\Rightarrow$) We demonstrate that if System 1 has a solution, then System 2 is inconsistent. Suppose that System 1 has a solution x_0, and that System 2 has a solution (u_0, v_0). Then we obtain $x_0^tA^tu_0 + x_0^tB^tv_0 = 0$, which results in a contradiction $(0 > x_0^tA^tu_0 = 0)$.

($\Leftarrow$) In this part we show that if System 1 has no solution, then System 2 has one. Hence suppose that System 1 is inconsistent, and consider two sets

$$S_1 = \{(z_1, z_2) : z_1 = Ax, z_2 = Bx, x\in E_n \}$$
$$S_2 = \{(z_1, z_2) : z_1 < 0, z_2 = 0\}.$$

Both sets S_1 and S_2 are nonempty and convex. Note that $S_1 \cap S_2 = \emptyset$, therefore, there exists a hyperplane separating the two sets. That is, there exists a nonzero vector (p_1, p_2) such that

$$p_1^tAx + p_2^tBx \geq p_1^tz_1 \text{ for any } (z_1, 0)\in clS_2 \text{ and for any } x\in E_n. \tag{1}$$

Note that $(0,0)\in cl\ S_2$, therefore, $p_1^tAx + p_2^tBx \geq 0$ for any $x\in E_n$. In particular, for $x = -(A^tp_1 + B^tp_2)$ we obtain $-(p_1^tA + p_2^tB)(A^tp_1 + B^tp_2) = -\|A^tp_1 + B^tp_2\|^2 \leq 0$, which necessarily yields

$$A^t p_1 + B^t p_2 = 0. \tag{2}$$

Next, let us remark that if $x = 0$, then equation (1) implies $0 \geq pz_1$ for any $z_1 < 0$. Therefore,

$$p_1 \geq 0. \tag{3}$$

It remains to show that $p_1 \neq 0$. Without loss of generality assume that $\text{rank}(B) = q$. If $p_1 = 0$ at

every solution to System 2, then $B^t p_2 = 0$, which yields $p_2 = 0$ since $\text{rank}(B) = q$. Therefore,

$$p_1 \neq 0. \tag{4}$$

Finally, note that by equations (2), (3) and (4), (p_1, p_2) is a solution to System 2. This completes

the proof. □

2.23. System 1: $Ax < 0$

System 2: $A^t p = 0,\ p \geq 0,\ p \neq 0$.

Consider the following pair of dual problems:

(L)   minimize $\{-c^t p:\ A^t p = 0,\ p \geq 0\}$

(D)   maximize $\{\ 0^t x:\ Ax \leq -c\}$,

and note that $p = 0$ is a feasible solution to (L).

If System 1 has a solution, then for any $c > 0$ problem (L) is unbounded, and consequently,

problem (D) has no feasible solution. This means that no vector x exists for which $Ax < 0$, hence

System 2 has no solution.

If System 2 has no solution, then for any $c > 0$ problem (L) has a unique optimal solution $p = 0$,

and therefore, problem (D) has an optimal solution. Therefore, there necessarily exists an x such

that $Ax < 0$. □

2.26. The proof is identical to that of Theorem 2.4.8 (take $p_1 = p$, and $p_2 = -p$).

2.35. a. Extreme points: all vectors (x_1, x_2, x_3) such that $x_1 = \frac{1}{2}(-1 \pm \sqrt{5-x_3})$, $x_2 = 1 - x_1 - x_3$,

and $x_3 \in (-\infty, 5/4]$.

Extreme directions: $d_1 = (0, 0, -1)$ and $d_2 = (0, 1, -1)$.

b. Extreme points: $(1, 0, 0)$, $(0, 1, 0)$, $(1, 0, 1)$ and $(0, 1, 1)$.

No extreme directions.

c. Extreme points: $(0, 0)$ and all points in E^2 that lie on the unit circle centered at the origin

between $\left(-\frac{\sqrt{2}}{2}, \frac{\sqrt{2}}{2}\right)$ and $\left(\frac{\sqrt{2}}{2}, \frac{\sqrt{2}}{2}\right)$, including the two end points.

No extreme directions.

2.46. The following result from linear algebra is very useful in this proof:

($*$) An $(m+1) \times (m+1)$ matrix G with a row of ones is invertible if and only if the remaining m

rows of G are linearly independent. In other words, if

$$G = \begin{bmatrix} B & a \\ e^t & 1 \end{bmatrix}, \text{ where B is an mxm matrix, a is an mx1 vector, e is a mx1 vector of ones,}$$

then G is invertible if and only if B is invertible.

Moreover, if G is invertible, then

$$G^{-1} = \begin{bmatrix} M & g \\ h^t & f \end{bmatrix}, \text{ where } M = B^{-1}(I + \frac{1}{\alpha}ae^tB^{-1}), \ g = -\frac{1}{\alpha}B^{-1}a, \ h^t = -\frac{1}{\alpha}e^tB^{-1}, \text{ and } f = \frac{1}{\alpha},$$

and where $\alpha = 1 - e^tB^{-1}a$.

By Theorem 2.6.4, an n-dimensional vector d is an extreme point of D if and only if matrix $\begin{bmatrix} A \\ e^t \end{bmatrix}$ can be decomposed into $[B_D \ N_D]$ such that $d = \begin{bmatrix} d_B \\ d_N \end{bmatrix}$, where $d_N = 0$ and $d_B = B_D^{-1}e_{m+1} \geq 0$. From property ($*$) above matrix $\begin{bmatrix} A \\ e^t \end{bmatrix}$ can be decomposed into $[B_D \ N_D]$, where B_D is a nonsingular matrix, if and only if A can be decomposed into $[B \ N]$, where B is an mxm invertible matrix. Matrix B_D must necessarily be of the form $\begin{bmatrix} B & a_j \\ e^t & 1 \end{bmatrix}$, where B is an mxm invertible submatrix of A. By applying equation for the inverse of G, we obtain

$$d_B = B_D^{-1} e_{m+1} = \begin{bmatrix} -\frac{1}{\alpha} B^{-1} a_j \\ \frac{1}{\alpha} \end{bmatrix} = \frac{1}{\alpha} \begin{bmatrix} -B^{-1} a_j \\ 1 \end{bmatrix},$$

where $\alpha = 1 - e_B^t B^{-1} a_j$. Notice that $d_B \geq 0$ if and only if $\alpha > 0$ and $B^{-1} a_j \leq 0$. This result together with Theorem 2.6.6 leads to the conclusion that d is an extreme point od D if and only if d is an extreme direction of S.   □

2.55. Problem P : minimize $\{c^t x : Ax = b, x \geq 0\}$.

(Homogeneous) Problem D : maximize $\{b^t y : A^t y \leq 0\}$.

Problem P has no feasible solution if and only if the system $Ax = b$, $x \geq 0$ is inconsistent. That is, by Farkas' Theorem, if and only if the system $A^t y \leq 0$, $b^t y > 0$ has a solution. Note that the system $A^t y \leq 0$, $b^t y > 0$ has a solution if and only if the homogeneous version of the dual problem is unbounded.   □

ANSWERS TO SELECTED EXERCISES

IN CHAPTER 3

3.3. a. $H = \begin{bmatrix} 2 & 2 \\ 2 & 0 \end{bmatrix}$ is not definite. Therefore, f(x) is neither convex nor concave.

b. $H(x) = e^{-(x_1+x_2)} \begin{bmatrix} x_1-2 & x_1-1 \\ x_1-1 & x_1 \end{bmatrix}$. Definiteness of the matrix H(x) depends on x. Therefore, f(x) is neither convex nor concave.

c. $-H = \begin{bmatrix} 2 & -2 \\ -2 & 10 \end{bmatrix}$ is positive definite. Therefore, f(x) is (strictly) concave.

d.

$H = \begin{bmatrix} 4 & 1 & -6 \\ 1 & 2 & 0 \\ -6 & 0 & 4 \end{bmatrix}$ is not definite. Therefore, f(x) is neither convex nor concave.

e.

$H = \begin{bmatrix} -2 & 4 & 2 \\ 4 & -6 & 4 \\ 2 & 4 & -4 \end{bmatrix}$ is not definite. Therefore, f(x) is neither convex nor concave.

3.5. $f(x) = 10-2(x_2-x_1^2)$, and its Hessian matrix is $H(x) = 4 \begin{bmatrix} -6x_1^2+2x_2 & 2x_1 \\ 2x_1 & -1 \end{bmatrix}$.

If $S = \{(x_1,x_2): -1 \leq x_1 \leq 1, -1 \leq x_2 \leq 1\}$, then H(x) is not definite on S, and therefore, f(x)

is neither convex nor concave on S.

If S is a convex set such that $S \subseteq \{(x_1, x_2): x_1^2 \geq x_2\}$, then H(x) is negative definite for all $x \in S$. Therefore, f(x) is strictly concave on S.

3.7. Let $x_1, x_2 \in S$, $\lambda \in (0,1)$, and let $x_\lambda = \lambda x_1 + (1-\lambda)x_2$. To establish convexity of f we need to show that $f(x_\lambda) - \lambda f(x_1) - (1-\lambda)f(x_2) \leq 0$. For notational convenience, let $D(x) = g(x_1)g(x_2) - \lambda g(x_\lambda)g(x_2) - (1-\lambda)g(x_\lambda)g(x_2)$. Under the assumption that g(x) > 0 for all $x \in S$, our task reduces to demonstrating that $D(x) \leq 0$ for any $x_1, x_2 \in S$, and any $\lambda \in (0,1)$. By concavity of g(x) we have

$$D(x) \leq g(x_1)g(x_2) - \lambda[\lambda g(x_1) + (1-\lambda)g(x_2)]g(x_2) - (1-\lambda)[\lambda g(x_1) + (1-\lambda)g(x_2)]g(x_1).$$

After rearrangement of terms on the right-hand side of this inequality we obtain

$$D(x) \leq -\lambda(1-\lambda)[g(x_1)^2 + g(x_2)^2] + 2\lambda(1-\lambda)g(x_1)g(x_2) =$$

$$= -\lambda(1-\lambda)[g(x_1)^2 + g(x_2)^2] + 2\lambda(1-\lambda)g(x_1)g(x_2) =$$

$$= -\lambda(1-\lambda)[g(x_1)^2 + g(x_2)^2 - 2g(x_1)g(x_2)] = -\lambda(1-\lambda)[g(x_1) - g(x_2)]^2.$$

Therefore, $D(x) \leq 0$ for any $x_1, x_2 \in S$ and any $\lambda \in (0,1)$, and thus f(x) is a convex function. $\square$

3.12. Let $x_1, x_2 \in S$, $\lambda \in (0,1)$, and let $x_\lambda = \lambda x_1 + (1-\lambda)x_2$. To establish convexity of h(.) we need to show that $h(x_\lambda) \leq \lambda h(x_1) + (1-\lambda)h(x_2)$. Notice that

$$h(x_\lambda) = g[f(x_\lambda)] \leq g[\lambda f(x_1) + (1-\lambda)f(x_2)] \leq \lambda g[f(x_1)] + (1-\lambda)g[f(x_2)] =$$

$$= \lambda h(x_1) + (1-\lambda)h(x_2).$$

In this derivation:

first and the last equality follow from the definition of h(x),

the first inequality follows from convexity of f(x) and monotonicity of g(y),

the second inequality follows from convexity of g(y).

This completes the proof. $\square$

3.13. Let x_1, x_2 be any two vectors from E^n, and let $\lambda \in [0, 1]$. Then, by definition of h(.), we obtain

$h(\lambda x_1 + (1-\lambda)x_2) = \lambda(Ax_1 + b) + (1-\lambda)(Ax_2 + b) = \lambda h(x_1) + (1-\lambda)h(x_2)$. Therefore,

$$f(\lambda x_1 + (1-\lambda)x_2) = g[h(\lambda x_1 + (1-\lambda)x_2)] = g[\lambda h(x_1) + (1-\lambda)h(x_2)]$$

$$\leq \lambda g[h(x_1)] + (1-\lambda)g[h(x_2)] = \lambda f(x_1) + (1-\lambda)f(x_2),$$

where inequality follows from the assumed convexity of $g(.)$. The foregoing derivation shows that $f(x)$ is convex. $\square$

By multivariate calculus we obtain $\nabla f(x) = A^t \nabla g[h(x)]$, and $H_f(x) = A^t H_g[h(x)]A$.

3.17. $f(x) = x^2(x^2 - 1)$ is strictly convex on the interval $[\,0.5, \infty)$, and on the interval $(-\infty, -0.5]$.

For all the remaining values for x, $f(x)$ is strictly concave.

3.20. Assume that $f(x)$ is convex. Then for any $\alpha \in (0, 1)$ and any x, y, we have

$$f(\alpha x + (1-\alpha)y) \leq \alpha f(x) + (1 - \alpha)f(y).$$

By the given definition of the gauge function, the right-hand side of this inequality can be rewritten as $f(\alpha x) + f((1-\alpha)y)$, which implies that $f(x)$ is subadditve. Proof of the reverse implication is similar. $\square$

3.24. First assume that $\overline{x} = 0$. Note that then $f(\overline{x}) = 0$ and $\xi^t \overline{x} = 0$ for any vector ξ in E_n.

($\Rightarrow$) If ξ is a subgradient of $f(x) = ||x||$ at 0, then we necessarily have $||x|| \geq \xi^t x$ for all $x \in E_n$. Thus in particular for $x = \xi$, we obtain $||\xi|| \geq ||\xi||^2$, which yields $||\xi|| \leq 1$.

($\Leftarrow$) Suppose that $||\xi|| \geq 1$. By the Schwarz inequality, we then obtain $\xi^t x \leq ||\xi|| \, ||x|| \leq ||x||$, thus ξ is a subgradient of $f(x) = ||x||$ at 0.

This completes the proof for the case when $\overline{x} = 0$. Now consider $\overline{x} \neq 0$.

($\Rightarrow$) Suppose that ξ is a subgradient of $f(x) = ||x||$ at $\overline{x}$. Then

$$||x|| - ||\overline{x}|| \geq \xi^t(x - \overline{x}) \text{ for all } x \in E_n. \tag{1}$$

In particular, the above inequality holds for $x = 0$, for $x = \lambda \overline{x}$, where $\lambda > 0$, and for $x = \xi$.

If $x = 0$, then $\xi^t \overline{x} \geq ||\overline{x}||$. Furthermore, by employing the Schwarz inequality we obtain

$$\|\overline{x}\| \leq \xi^t\overline{x} \leq \|\xi\| \, \|\overline{x}\|.$$

If $x = \lambda\overline{x}$, $\lambda > 0$, then $\|x\| = \lambda\|\overline{x}\|$, and equation (1) yields $(\lambda - 1)\|\overline{x}\| \geq (\lambda - 1)\xi^t\overline{x}$. If $\lambda > 1$, then $\|\overline{x}\| \geq \xi^t\overline{x}$, and if $\lambda < 1$, then $\|\overline{x}\| \leq \xi^t\overline{x}$. Therefore, in either case, if ξ is a subgradient at $\overline{x}$, then it must satisfy the equation

$$\xi^t\overline{x} = \|\overline{x}\|.$$

Finally, if $x = \xi$, then equation (1) results in $\|\xi\| - \|\overline{x}\| \geq \xi^t\xi - \xi^t\overline{x}$. However, by the necessary condition we have $\xi^t\overline{x} = \|\overline{x}\|$, therefore $\|\xi\|(1 - \|\xi\|) \geq 0$. This yields

$$1 - \|\xi\| \geq 0.$$

Combining the three necessary conditions together, we conclude that if ξ is a subgradient of $f(x) = \|x\|$ at $\overline{x} \neq 0$, then $\xi^t\overline{x} = \|\overline{x}\|$ and $\|\xi\| = 1$.

($\Leftarrow$) Consider a vector $\xi \in E_n$ such that $\|\xi\| = 1$ and $\xi^t\overline{x} = \|\overline{x}\|$. Then $f(x) - f(\overline{x}) - \xi^t(x - \overline{x}) = \|x\| - \|\overline{x}\| - \xi^t(x - \overline{x}) = \|\overline{x}\| - \xi^t\overline{x} \geq \|\overline{x}\| \, (1 - \|\xi\|) = 0$. Again the Schwarz inequality ($\xi^t\overline{x} \leq \|\xi\| \, \|\overline{x}\|$) was applied to derive the last inequality. Thus ξ is a subgradient of $f(x) = \|x\|$ at $\overline{x} \neq 0$. This completes the proof. $\quad\square$

In order to derive the gradient of $f(x)$ at $\overline{x} \neq 0$, notice that $\|\xi\| = 1$ and $\xi^t\overline{x} = \|\overline{x}\|$ if and only if $\xi = \frac{1}{\|\overline{x}\|}\overline{x}$. Thus $\nabla f(\overline{x}) = \frac{1}{\|\overline{x}\|}\overline{x}$.

3.26. a. See Theorem 6.3.1 and its proof.

b. For a given vector $\overline{u}$, let $X(\overline{u}) = \{x_1, ..., x_k\}$ denote the set of all vertices of set X that are optimal solutions for the problem minimize $\{c^tx + \overline{u}^t(Ax - b): x \in X\}$. Then $\xi(\overline{u})$ is a subgradient of $\theta(u)$ at $\overline{u}$ if and only if $\xi(\overline{u})$ is in a convex hull of $Ax_1 - b, ..., Ax_k - b$, where $x_i \in X(\overline{u})$ for $i = 1, ..., k$. That is, $\xi(\overline{u})$ is a subgradient of $\theta(u)$ at $\overline{u}$ if and only if $\xi(\overline{u}) = A\sum_{i=1}^{k} \lambda_i x_i - b$ for some nonnegative $\lambda_1, ..., \lambda_k$, such that $\sum_{i=1}^{k} \lambda_i = 1$. Also see Theorem 6.3.7.

3.30. Function $f(x) = x^tAx$ can be represented in a more convenient form as $f(x) = \frac{1}{2}x^t(A + A^t)x$. The Hessian matrix of $f(x)$ is $H = A + A^t$. H is positive semidefinite if and only if $\theta \geq 2$, and is positive definite for $\theta > 2$. Therefore, if $\theta > 2$, then f(x) is strictly convex. To examine the case when $\theta = 2$, consider the following three points $x_1 = (1, \ 0, \ 0)$ and $x_2 = (0, \ 0, \ 1)$, and $\overline{x} = \frac{1}{2}x_1 + \frac{1}{2}x_2$. As a result of direct substitution we obtain $f(x_1) = f(x_2) = 4$, and $f(\overline{x}) = 4$. This shows that f(x) is not strictly convex (though it is still convex) when $\theta = 2$.

3.35. Matrix H is symmetric, and therefore, it is diagonalizable. That is, there exists an orthogonal nxn matrix Q, and a diagonal nxn matrix D such that $H = QDQ^t$. Columns of matrix Q are simply normalized eigenvectors of matrix H, and diagonals of matrix D are eigenvalues of H. By positive semidefiniteness of matrix H we have $D \geq 0$, and hence there exists a square root matrix $D^{1/2}$ of D (that is $D = D^{1/2}D^{1/2}$).

If $x = 0$, then readily $Hx = 0$. Suppose that $x^tHx = 0$ for some $x \neq 0$. Below we show that then Hx is necessarily 0. For notational convenience let $z = D^{1/2}Q^tx$. Then the following equations are equivalent to $x^tHx = 0$:

$$x^tQD^{1/2}D^{1/2}Q^tx = 0$$

$$z^tz = 0$$

$$z = 0.$$

By premultiplying the last equation by $QD^{1/2}$ we obtain $QD^{1/2}z = 0$, which by the definition of z gives $QDQ^tx = 0$. Thus $Hx = 0$, which completes the proof. $\qquad\square$

3.42. Suppose that λ_1 and λ_2 are in the interval $(0, \ \delta)$, and such that $\lambda_2 > \lambda_1$. We need to show that $f(x+\lambda_2 d) \geq g(x+\lambda_1 d)$.

Let $\alpha = \lambda_1/\lambda_2$. Note that $\alpha \in (0, \ 1)$, and $x + \lambda_1 d = \alpha(x + \lambda_2 d) + (1-\alpha)x$. Therefore, by convexity of function f(x) we obtain $f(x+\lambda_1 d) \leq \alpha f(x+\lambda_2 d) + (1-\alpha)f(x)$, which leads to $f(x+\lambda_1 d) \leq f(x+\lambda_2 d)$ since, by assumption, $f(x) \leq f(x+\lambda d)$ for any $\lambda \in (0, \ \delta)$.

For strict convexity case, replace weak inequalities with strict inequalities to conclude that $f(x+\lambda d)$ is strictly increasing over the interval $(0, \ \delta)$. $\qquad\square$

3.43. ($\Rightarrow$)Vector d is a descent direction of f(x) at $\overline{x}$, hence $f(\overline{x}+\lambda d)-f(\overline{x}) < 0$ for all $\lambda \in (0, \delta)$. Moreover, f(x) is a convex and differentiable function, hence $f(\overline{x}+\lambda d)-f(\overline{x}) \geq \lambda \nabla f(\overline{x})^t d$. Therefore, $\nabla f(\overline{x})^t d < 0$.

($\Leftarrow$) See the proof of Theorem 4.1.2. $\square$

Note: If function f(x) is not convex, then it is not true that $\nabla f(\overline{x})^t d < 0$ whenever d is a descent direction of f(x) at $\overline{x}$.

3.44. Result follows directly from Exercise 3.43.

3.47. For notational convenience let $g(x) = c_1^t x + \alpha_1$, and let $h(x) = c_2^t x + \alpha_2$. In order to prove pseudoconvexity of $f(x) = \dfrac{g(x)}{h(x)}$ on the set $S = \{x: h(x) > 0\}$ we need to show that for any $x_1, x_2 \in S$ if $\nabla f(x_1)^t (x_2 - x_1) \geq 0$, then $f(x_2) \geq f(x_1)$.

Assume that $\nabla f(x_1)^t (x_2 - x_1) \geq 0$ for some $x_1, x_2 \in S$. By the definition of f(.) we have $\nabla f(x) = \dfrac{1}{[h(x)]^2}[(c_1 c_2^t - c_2 c_1^t)x + c_1 \alpha_2 - c_2 \alpha_1]$, therefore, our assumption yields

$[(c_1 c_2^t - c_2 c_1^t)x_1 + c_1 \alpha_2 - c_2 \alpha_1]^t (x_2 - x_1) \geq 0$. Rearrangement of terms in the last inequality results in $[h(x_1)c_1 - g(x_1)c_2]^t(x_2 - x_1) \geq 0$. Furthermore, by adding and subtracting $\alpha_1 h(x_1) + \alpha_2 g(x_1)$ we obtain $g(x_2)h(x_1) - h(x_2)g(x_1) \geq 0$. Finally, by dividing this inequality by $h(x_1)h(x_2)$ (>0), we obtain $f(x_2) \geq f(x_1)$, which completes the proof of pseudoconvexity of f(x). Pseudoconcavity of f(x) on S can be shown in a similar way. $\square$

3.52. Let $x_1, x_2 \in E_n$. Without loss of generality assume that $h(x_1) \geq h(x_2)$. Since function g(.) is nondecreasing, the foregoing assumption implies that $g[h(x_1)] \geq g[h(x_2)]$, or equivalently, that $f(x_1) \geq f(x_2)$. By quasiconvexity of function h(.), we have $h(\alpha x_1 + (1-\alpha)x_2) \leq h(x_1)$ for any $\alpha \in (0, 1)$. Function g(.) is nondecreasing, therefore, $f(\alpha x_1 + (1-\alpha)x_2) = g[h(\alpha x_1 + (1-\alpha)x_2)] \leq g[h(x_1)] = f(x_1)$. This shows that f(x) is quasiconvex. $\square$

3.57. Let α be an arbitrary real number, and let $S = \{ x: f(x) \leq \alpha \}$. Furthermore, let x_1 and x_2 be any two elements of S. We need to show that S is a convex set, that is, $f(\lambda x_1 + (1-\lambda)x_2) \leq \alpha$ for any $\lambda \in (0, 1)$. By definition of $f(x)$ we have

$$f(\lambda x_1 + (1-\lambda)x_2) = \frac{g(\lambda x_1 + (1-\lambda)x_2)}{h(\lambda x_1 + (1-\lambda)x_2)} \leq \frac{\lambda g(x_1) + (1-\lambda)g(x_2)}{\lambda h(x_1) + (1-\lambda)h(x_2)},$$

where the inequality follows from the assumed properties of functions $g(.)$ and $h(.)$. Furthermore, since $f(x_1) \leq \alpha$, an d $f(x_2) \leq \alpha$, we obtain

$$\lambda g(x_1) \leq \lambda \alpha h(x_1) \text{ and } (1-\lambda)g(x_2) \leq (1-\lambda)\alpha h(x_2).$$

By adding the two inequalities we obtain $\lambda g(x_1) + (1-\lambda)g(x_2) \leq \alpha[\lambda h(x_1) + (1-\lambda)h(x_2)]$. Since $h(.)$ is assumed to be a positive-valued function, the last inequalities yields

$$\frac{\lambda g(x_1) + (1-\lambda)g(x_2)}{\lambda h(x_1) + (1-\lambda)h(x_2)} \leq \alpha.$$

Thus, S is a convex set, and therefore, $f(x)$ is a quasiconvex function. $\square$

3.58. We need to prove that if $g(x)$ is a convex nonnegative-valued function on S and $h(x)$ is a concave and positive-valued function on S, then $f(x) = g(x)/h(x)$ is a quasiconvex function on S. For this purpose we show that for any $x_1, x_2 \in S$, if $f(x_1) \geq f(x_2)$, then $f(x_\lambda) \leq f(x_1)$, where $x_\lambda = \lambda x_1 + (1-\lambda)x_2$, and $\lambda \in (0, 1)$. Note that by the definition of $f(.)$ and assumption that $h(x) > 0$ for all $x \in S$, it suffices to show that $g(x_\lambda)h(x_1) - g(x_1)h(x_\lambda) \leq 0$. Towards this end, observe that

$g(x_\lambda)h(x_1) \leq [\lambda g(x_1) + (1-\lambda)g(x_2)]h(x_1)$ since $g(x)$ is convex and $h(x) > 0$ on S,

$g(x_1)h(x_\lambda) \geq g(x_1)[\lambda h(x_1) + (1-\lambda)h(x_2)]$ since $h(x)$ is convex and $g(x) \leq 0$ on S,

$g(x_2)h(x_1) - g(x_1)h(x_2) \leq 0$, since $f(x_1) \geq f(x_2)$ and $h(x) > 0$ on S.

From the foregoing inequalities we obtain

$$g(x_\lambda)h(x_1) - g(x_1)h(x_\lambda) \leq [\lambda g(x_1) + (1-\lambda)g(x_2)]h(x_1) - g(x_1)[\lambda h(x_1) + (1-\lambda)h(x_2)]$$

$$= (1-\lambda)[g(x_2)h(x_1) - g(x_1)h(x_2)] \leq 0,$$

which implies that $f(x_\lambda) \leq \max\{f(x_1), f(x_2)\} = f(x_1)$. $\square$

3.59. By assumption, $h(x) \neq 0$, hence function $f(x)$ can be rewritten as $f(x) = g(x)/p(x)$, where $p(x) = 1/h(x)$. Furthermore, since $h(x)$ is a concave and positive-valued function, we conclude that $p(x)$ is convex and positive-valued on S. Therefore, result given in Exercise 3.58 applies. This completes the proof. $\qquad\square$

3.60. If $g(x)$ and $h(x)$ are differentiable, then the function defined in Exercise 3.58 is pseudoconvex. To prove it we show that for any $x_1, x_2 \in S$, if $\nabla f(x_1)^t(x_2 - x_1) \geq 0$, then $f(x_2) \geq f(x_1)$. From the rules for differentiating and the assumption $h(x) > 0$ it follows that $\nabla f(x_1)^t(x_2 - x_1) \geq 0$ if and only if $[h(x_1)\nabla g(x_1) - g(x_1)\nabla h(x_1)]^t(x_2 - x_1) \geq 0$. Furthermore, note that

$\nabla g(x_1)^t(x_2 - x_1) \leq g(x_2) - g(x_1)$, since $g(x)$ is a convex and differentiable function on S, and

$\nabla h(x_1)^t(x_2 - x_1) \geq h(x_2) - h(x_1)$, since $h(x)$ is a concave and differentiable function on S.

By multiplying the latter inequality by $-g(x_1) \leq 0$, and the former one by $h(x_1) > 0$, and adding the resulting inequalities, we obtain (after rearrangement of terms):

$$[h(x_1)\nabla g(x_1) - g(x_1)\nabla h(x_1)]^t(x_2 - x_1) \leq h(x_1)g(x_2) - g(x_1)h(x_2).$$

The left-hand side expression is nonnegative by our assumption, and therefore, $h(x_1)g(x_2) - g(x_1)h(x_2) \geq 0$, which implies $f(x_2) \geq f(x_1)$. This completes the proof. $\qquad\square$

3.65. a. See the answer to Exercise 6.7.

b. If $y_1 \leq y_2$, then $\{x: g(x) \leq y_1, x \in S\} \subseteq \{x: g(x) \leq y_2, x \in S\}$, hence $\phi(y_1) \geq \phi(y_2)$.

3.66. See the answer to Exercise 6.7.

ANSWERS TO SELECTED EXERCISES

IN CHAPTER 4

4.1. Let $f(x) = x_1^2 - x_1 x_2 + 2x_2^2 - 2x_1 + e^{x_1 + x_2}$.

a. The first-order necessary condition is $\nabla f(x) = 0$, that is:

$$2x_1 - x_2 + e^{x_1 + x_2} = 2$$

$$-x_1 + 4x_2 + e^{x_1 + x_2} = 0.$$

The Hessian H of $f(x)$ is $H = \begin{bmatrix} 2 + e^{x_1 + x_2} & e^{x_1 + x_2} - 1 \\ e^{x_1 + x_2} - 1 & 4 + e^{x_1 + x_2} \end{bmatrix}$, and as can be easily verified, H is a positive definite matrix. Therefore, the first-order necessary condition is sufficient in this case.

b. $\bar{x} = (0, 0)$ is not an optimal solution. $\nabla f(\bar{x}) = [\begin{array}{cc} -1 & 1 \end{array}]^t$, and any direction $d = (d_1, d_2)$ such that $-d_1 + d_2 < 0$ is a descent direction of $f(x)$ at $\bar{x}$.

c. Let us select $d = (1, 0)$. Then $f(\bar{x} + \lambda d) = \lambda^2 - 2\lambda + e^\lambda$. The minimum value of $f(\bar{x} + \lambda d)$ over the interval $[0, \infty)$ is .839484301 and is attained at $\lambda^* = .3149$.

d. If the last term is dropped, $f(x) = x_1^2 - x_1 x_2 + 2x_2^2 - 2x_1$. Then the first-order necessary condition yields a unique solution $\bar{x}_1 = 8/7$ and $\bar{x}_2 = 2/7$. Again, the Hessian of $f(x)$ is positive definite, so that the foregoing values of x_1 and x_2 are optimal. The minimum value of $f(x)$ is then $-56/49$.

4.4. a. In general, the problem seeks a vector y in the column space of A $(y = Ax)$ that is the closest to the given vector b. If b is in the column space of A, then we need to find a solution of the system $Ax = b$. If in addition to it, the rank of A is n, then x is unique. If b is not in the column space of A, then a vector in the column space of A that is the closest to b is the projection vector of b onto the column space of A. In this case, the problem seeks a solution of the system $Ax = y$, where y is the projection vector of b onto the column space of A.

In answers to parts (b), (c) and (d) below it is assumed that b is not in the column space of A, since otherwise the problem trivially reduces to "find a solution to the system $Ax = b$".

b. Assume that $||.||_2$ is used, and let $f(x)$ denote the objective function in this optimization problem. Then, $f(x) = b^t b - 2x^t A^t b + x^t A^t A x$, and the first order necessary condition is $A^t A x = A^t b$. The Hessian matrix of $f(x)$ is $A^t A$, which is positive semidefinite. Therefore, $f(x)$ is a convex function. By Theorem 3.4.3 it then follows that the necessary condition is also sufficient for optimality.

c. The number of optimal solutions is exactly the same as the number of solutions of the system $A^t A x = A^t b$.

d. If rank of A is n, then $A^t A$ is positive definite and invertible. In this case $x = (A^t A)^{-1} A^t b$ is the unique solution. If rank of A is less than n, then the system $A^t A x = A^t b$ has infinitely many solutions. In this case additional criteria can be used to select a unique optimal solution, if such is needed. For details see *Linear Algebra and Its Applications* by Gilbert Strang. Harcourt Brace Jovanovich, Publishers, San Diego, 1988, Third Edition.

e. Rank of A is 3, therefore, a unique solution exists. $(A^t A)^{-1} = \frac{1}{4} \begin{bmatrix} 8 & -4 & -8 \\ -4 & 3 & 5 \\ -8 & 5 & 11 \end{bmatrix}$, and $A^t b =$ $[2 \ 1 \ 1]^t$. The unique solution is $x^* = [\ 1 \ \ 0 \ \ 0\ ]^t$.

4.6. Switch to minimization of the function $f(x_1, x_2) = -x_1^2 - 4x_1 x_2 - x_2^2$.

a. The KKT system is as follows:

$$
\begin{aligned}
-2x_1 \quad -4x_2 \quad +2vx_1 \quad &= 0 \\
-4x_1 \quad -2x_2 \quad +2vx_2 \quad &= 0 \\
x_1^2 \quad +x_2^2 \qquad\qquad &= 1.
\end{aligned}
$$

There are four solutions to this system:

$$(x_1, x_2) = (\ \sqrt{2}/2, \ \sqrt{2}/2), \text{ and } v = 3$$

$(x_1, x_2) = (-\sqrt{2}/2, -\sqrt{2}/2)$, and $v = 3$

$(x_1, x_2) = (\sqrt{2}/2, -\sqrt{2}/2)$, and $v = -1$

$(x_1, x_2) = (-\sqrt{2}/2, \sqrt{2}/2)$, and $v = -1$.

The objective function $f(x_1, x_2)$ takes on the value of -3 at the first two points, and the value of 1 at the remaining two.

There are two optimal solutions $\overline{x}_1 = (\sqrt{2}/2, \sqrt{2}/2)$ and $\overline{x}_2 = (-\sqrt{2}/2, -\sqrt{2}/2)$. To support this statement, one can use graphical display, or second order sufficiency conditions given in part (b) below, or show that the given problem is equivalent to minimize $\{(x_1-x_2)^2 : x_1^2 + x_2^2 = 1\}$, whose optimal solutions are $\overline{x}_1$ and $\overline{x}_2$.

b. $L(x) = -x_1^2 - 4x_1x_2 - x_2^2 + v(x_1^2 + x_2^2 - 1)$, therefore,

$$\nabla^2 L(x) = 2 \begin{bmatrix} v-1 & -2 \\ -2 & v-1 \end{bmatrix}.$$

At $v = 3$, $\nabla^2 L(x)$ is a positive definite matrix and therefore, $\overline{x}_1 = (\sqrt{2}/2, \sqrt{2}/2)$ and $\overline{x}_2 = (-\sqrt{2}/2, -\sqrt{2}/2)$ are both strict local optima.

c. See answers to parts (a) and (b).

4. 8. a. The KKT system for the given problem is:

$$2x_1 + 2u_1x_1 + u_2 - u_3 \qquad = 9/2$$

$$2x_2 - u_1 + u_2 \qquad - u_4 = 4$$

$$x_1^2 - x_2 \leq 0$$

$$x_1 + x_2 \leq 6$$

$$u_1(x_1^2 - x_2) = 0, \quad u_2(6 - x_1 - x_2) = 0, \quad x_1u_3 = 0, \; x_1u_4 = 0$$

$$x_1 \geq 0, \; x_2 \geq 0, \; u_i \geq 0 \text{ for } i = 1, 2, 3, 4.$$

At $\overline{x} = (3/2, \; 9/4)$ we necessarily have $\overline{u}_2 = \overline{u}_3 = \overline{u}_4 = 0$, which yields a unique value for u_2, namely, $\overline{u}_2 = 1/2$. The above values for x_1, x_2, and u_i for $i = 1, 2, 3, 4$ solve the KKT system, therefore, $\bar{x}$ is a KKT point.

b. Graphical illustration:

From the graph below it follows that at $\bar{x}$ the gradient of $f(x)$ is a negative multiple of the gradient of $g_1(x) = x_2 - x_1^2$, the only binding constraint function at $\bar{x}$.

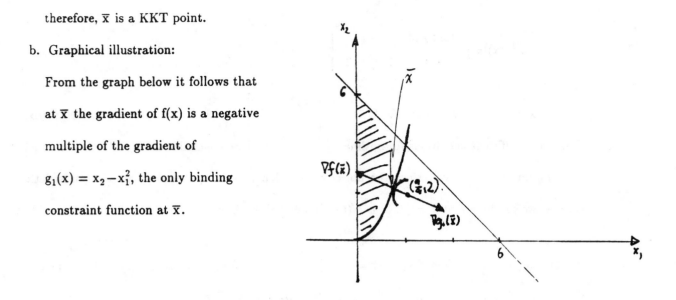

c. It can be easily verified that $\bar{x} = (3/2,\ 9/4)$ is a local minimizer in this problem. Moreover, the objective function is strictly convex, and the binding constraint functions are convex. Therefore, $\bar{x}$ is the unique (global) optimal solution to this problem.

4.10. The KKT system is:

$$4x_1^3 + 24x_1 - x_2 - u_1 - 2u_2 - u_3 = 1$$

$$4x_2^3 + 12x_2 - x_1 - u_1 + u_2 - u_4 = 1$$

$$x_1 + x_2 \geq 6$$

$$2x_1 - x_2 \geq 3$$

$$u_1(6 - x_1 - x_2) = 0, \qquad u_2(3 - 2x_1 + x_2) = 0$$

$$u_3 x_1 = 0,\ \ u_4 x_2 = 0,$$

$$x_1 \geq 0,\ x_2 \geq 0,\ u_i \geq 0 \text{ for } i = 1, 2, 3, 4.$$

If $\bar{x} = (3,\ 3)$, then $\bar{u}_3 = \bar{u}_4 = 0$. Consequently, the first two equations give $\bar{u}_1 = 152$ and $\bar{u}_2 = 12$. Thus, all Lagrangian multipliers are nonnegative, which shows that $\bar{x} = (3,\ 3)$ is a KKT point. The Hessian matrix $\nabla^2 L(x)$ of the restricted Lagrangian is

$$\nabla^2 L(x) = \begin{bmatrix} 12x_1^2+24 & -1 \\ -1 & 12x_2^2+12 \end{bmatrix},$$

and at $\bar{x} = (3, 3)$ we obtain $\nabla^2 L(\bar{x}) = \begin{bmatrix} 132 & -1 \\ -1 & 120 \end{bmatrix}$, which is a positive definite matrix. Therefore, sufficient conditions for optimality are met, and we conclude that $\bar{x} = (3, 3)$ is a strict local minimizer. Moreover, since the objective function in this optimization problem is strictly convex, we conclude that $\bar{x} = (3, 3)$ is a (unique) global minimizer.

4.15. a. The objective function $f(x_1, x_2) = \dfrac{x_1+3x_2 +3}{2x_1+ x_2 + 6}$ is pseudoconvex on the feasible region. Constraint functions are linear, hence both quasiconvex, and quasiconcave. Therefore, by Theorem 4.3.8, if $\bar{x}$ is a KKT point for this problem, then $\bar{x}$ is a global optimal solution.

b. First note that $f(0,0) = f(6,0) = 1/2$, and moreover $f(\lambda(0,0) + (1-\lambda)(6,0)) = 1/2$ for any $\lambda \in [0,1]$. Since $(0, 0)$ and $(6, 0)$ are feasible solutions, and the feasible region is a polyhedral set, any convex combination of $(0, 0)$ and $(6, 0)$ is also a feasible solution. It thus remains to show that one of the two points is a KKT point. Consider $(6, 0)$. as a result of substituting $(6, 0)$ for (x_1, x_2) into the KKT system

$$\frac{-5x_2}{(2x_1+x_2+6)^2} + 2u_1 - u_2 - u_3 \qquad = 0$$

$$\frac{5x_1+15}{(2x_1+x_2+6)^2} + u_1 + 2u_2 \qquad - u_4 \quad = 0$$

$$2x_1 + x_2 \leq 12$$

$$-x_1 + 2x_2 \leq 4$$

$x_1 \geq 0,\ x_2 \geq 0,\ u_i \geq 0$ for $i = 1, 2, 3, 4$

$u_1(2x_1 + x_2 -12) = 0,\ u_2(-x_1 + 2x_2 - 4) = 0,\ u_3x_1 = 0,\ u_4x_2 = 0,$

we obtain unique values for Lagrangian multipliers: $u_1=u_2=u_3= 0$, and $u_4 = 5/36$. Since $u_i \geq 0$, $i = 1, 2, 3, 4$, we conclude that $(6, 0)$ is indeed a KKT point, and therefore, by part (a), it solves the given problem. By earlier derivation, any point between (0, 0) and (6, 0) is an optimal solution.

4.17. a. In order to determine whether a point $\bar{x}$ is a KKT point one needs to solve the KKT system:

$$\nabla f(\bar{x}) + \sum_{i \in I} \nabla g_i(\bar{x}) u_i = 0 \ , \ u_i \geq 0, \ i \in I,$$

where I is the set of indices of constraints active at $\bar{x}$.

Let $c = -\nabla f(\bar{x})$ and let $A = [\nabla g_i(\bar{x})]_{i \in I}$. Then KKT system can be rewritten as

$$Au = c, \quad u \geq 0. \tag{1}$$

Therefore, $\bar{x}$ is a KKT point if and only if the system (1) has a solution. Note that system (1) is linear, and it has a solution if and only if the optimal objective value in the problem

$$\text{minimize} \quad e^t y$$

$$\text{subject to} \quad Au + y = c$$

$$u \geq 0, y \geq 0,$$

where e^t is a column vector of ones, is zero. Vector y in this problem is a vector of artificial variables, and the problem itself is Phase One LP for finding a nonnegative solution to Au=c.

b. In the presence of constraints $h_i(x) = 0$, i = 1, ..., l, the KKT system is

$$\nabla f(\bar{x}) + \sum_{i \in I} \nabla g_i(\bar{x}) u_i + \sum_{i=1}^{l} \nabla h_i(\bar{x}) v_i = 0 \ , \ u_i \geq 0, \ i \in I,$$

where I is the set of indices of constraints active at $\bar{x}$. Let A be as defined in part (a), and let $B = [\nabla h_i(\bar{x})]$ be an nx$l$ matrix. Then the corresponding Phase One problem is:

$$\text{minimize} \quad e^t y$$

$$\text{subject to} \quad Au + Bv + y = c$$

$$u \geq 0, y \geq 0.$$

c. In this example we have $\bar{x} = (1, 2, 5)$, $c = -\nabla f(\bar{x}) = -(8, 3, 23)^t$. Furthermore, I = {1, 3}, therefore, $A = [\nabla g_1(\overline{x})\ \nabla g_3(\overline{x})] = \begin{bmatrix} 2 & -1 \\ 4 & -1 \\ -1 & 0 \end{bmatrix}$. Thus, $\overline{x} = (1, 2, 5)$ is a KKT point if and only

if the optimal objective value in the problem

$$\begin{array}{lll}
\text{minimize} & y_1 + y_2 + y_3 \\
\text{subject to} & -2u_1 + u_3 + y_1 & = 8 \\
& -4u_1 + u_3 \qquad + y_2 & = 3 \\
& u_1 \qquad\qquad\qquad + y_3 = 23 \\
& u_1 \geq 0,\ u_3 \geq 0,\ y_i \geq 0,\ i = 1, 2, 3
\end{array}$$

is zero. However, the optimal solution to this problem is $\overline{u}_1 = 2.5$, $\overline{u}_3 = 13$, $\overline{y}_1 = \overline{y}_2 = 0$, $\overline{y}_3 = 20.5$, and the optimal objective value is positive (20.5), therefore, we conclude that $\overline{x} = (1, 2, 5)$ is not a KKT point.

4.18. a. $d = 0$ is a feasible solution and it gives the objective function value equal to 0. Therefore, $\overline{z} \leq 0$.

b. If $\overline{z} < 0$, then $\nabla f(\overline{x})^t \overline{d} < 0$. By Theorem 4.1.2, $\overline{d}$ is a descent direction. Furthermore, by concavity of $g_i(x)$ at $\overline{x}$, $i \in I$, there exists $\delta > 0$ such that $g_i(\overline{x} + \lambda\overline{d}) \leq \lambda \nabla g_i(\overline{x})\overline{d}$ for $\lambda \in (0, \delta)$. Since vector $\overline{d}$ is a feasible solution to the given problem, we necessarily have $\nabla g_i(\overline{x})\overline{d} \leq 0$ for $i \in I$, and thus $g_i(\overline{x} + \lambda\overline{d}) \leq 0$ for $\lambda \in (0, \delta)$. All the remaining constraint functions are continuous at $\overline{x}$, hence again there exists $\delta_1 > 0$ such that $g_i(\overline{x} + \lambda\overline{d}) \leq 0$ for $\lambda \in (0, \delta_1)$. This shows that $\overline{d}$ is a feasible and descent direction of $f(x)$ at $\overline{x}$.

c. If $\overline{z} = 0$, then the dual of the (linear) problem has an optimal solution, and the optimal dual objective function value is also 0. The dual problem can be formulated in the following way:

$$\begin{array}{ll}
\text{maximize} & -v_1 - v_2 \\
\text{subject to} & -\sum_{i \in I} \nabla g_i(\overline{x})u_i - v_1 + v_2 = \nabla f(\overline{x}) \\
& u_i \geq 0,\ i \in I,\ v_1 \geq 0,\ v_2 \geq 0.
\end{array}$$

Thus if $\overline{z} = 0$, then v_1 and v_2 are necessarily equal to 0 at an optimal dual solution. If so, then there exist nonnegative numbers u_i, $i \in I$ such that $\nabla f(\overline{x}) + \sum_{i \in I} \nabla g_i(\overline{x})u_i = 0$. Thus, $\overline{x}$ satisfies the

KKT conditions.

4.19. Substitute $y = x - \overline{x}$ to obtain an equivalent form of problem $\overline{P}$:

$$\text{minimize } \{ \, \| \, y - d \, \|^2 : Ay = 0 \}.$$

a. Problem $\overline{P}$ seeks a vector in the nullspace of A that is closest to the given vector d, that is to the vector $-\nabla f(\overline{x})$. Since rank of A is m, an optimal solution to the problem $\overline{P}$ is the orthogonal projection vector of $-\nabla f(\overline{x})$ onto the nullspace of A.

b. The KKT conditions are:

$$x + A^t v = \overline{x} - d$$
$$Ax \qquad = b.$$

The objective function in $\overline{P}$ is strictly convex, and the constraints are linear, therefore, the KKT conditions for problem $\overline{P}$ are both necessary and sufficient for optimality.

c. If $\overline{x}$ is a KKT point for problem $\overline{P}$, then there exists a vector $\overline{v}$ of Lagrange multipliers associated with equations $Ax = b$, such that

$$A^t \overline{v} = d, \text{ that is, } \nabla f(\overline{x}) + A^t \overline{v} = 0.$$

Then, $\overline{x}$ is a KKT point for problem P if $\overline{v} \geq 0$.

d. $\hat{x} = \overline{x} - d + A^t (AA^t)^{-1} d$. Also, see the answer to Exercise 11.20.

4.23. Assume that $c \neq 0$.

a. Let $f(d) = -c^t d$, and $g(d) = d^t d - 1$. The KKT system is as follows:

$$-c + 2du = 0$$
$$d^t d \qquad \leq 1$$
$$u(d^t d - 1) = 0$$
$$u \geq 0.$$

$\overline{d} = c / \|c\|$ is a KKT point. To verify it substitute $\overline{d}$ for d and $\|c\|/2$ for u into the foregoing system. Moreover, $\overline{d}$ is an optimal solution, because it is a KKT point, and sufficiency conditions for optimality are met ($f(d)$ is a linear function, hence, pseudoconvex, and $g(d)$ is a convex function, hence it is quasiconvex).

Vector $\overline{d}$ is the unique global optimal solution. The KKT system provides necessary and sufficient conditions for optimality in this case, and $\overline{d} = c/\|c\|$, $\overline{u} = \|c\|/2$ is its unique solution. To support this statement, notice that if $u > 0$, then $d^t d = 1$, which together with the first equation results in $d = c/\|c\|$, and $u = \|c\|/2$. If $u = 0$, then the first equation is inconsistent regardless of what vector d is.

b. The steepest ascent direction of a differentiable function $f(x)$ at $\overline{x}$ can be found as an optimal solution $\overline{d}$ to the following problem:

$$\text{maximize } \{\nabla f(\overline{x})^t d : d^t d \leq 1\},$$

which is identical to the problem considered in part (a) with $c = \nabla f(\overline{x})$. Thus, if $\nabla f(\overline{x}) \neq 0$, then the steepest ascent direction is $\overline{d} = \nabla f(\overline{x})/\|\nabla f(\overline{x})\|$.

4.24. Let $y_j = \frac{a_j}{b} x_j$ and $d_j = \frac{c_j a_j}{b}$ for $j = 1, ..., n$. Then the given optimization problem is equivalent to the following one:

$$\text{minimize } \sum_{j=1}^{n} \frac{d_j}{y_j}$$
$$\text{subject to } \quad \sum_{j=1}^{n} y_j = 1$$
$$y_j \geq 0 \text{ for } j = 1, ..., n.$$

The KKT system for the above problem is

$$-\frac{d_j}{y_j^2} - u_j + v = 0 \quad \text{for } j = 1, ..., n$$

$$u_j y_j = 0, u_j \geq 0, \ y_j \geq 0 \ \text{ for } j = 1, ..., n.$$

Readily, for each $j = 1, ..., n$, y_j must take on a positive value, and hence $u_j = 0$. Then the KKT system gives $v = \sum_{j=1}^{n} \frac{d_j}{y_j}$. By substituting this expression for v into each of the first n equations we obtain $\overline{y}_j = \dfrac{\sqrt{d_j}}{\sum\limits_{j=1}^{n}\sqrt{d_j}}$, $j = 1, ..., n$. This gives a unique KKT point for the transformed problem.

The unique KKT point for the original problem is $\overline{x}_j = \dfrac{b\sqrt{a_jc_j}}{a_j\sum\limits_{j=1}^{n}\sqrt{a_jc_j}}$, $j = 1, ..., n$.

4.25. Consider the problem

$$\text{minimize} \quad \sum_{j=1}^{n} x_j$$

$$\text{subject to} \quad \prod_{j=1}^{n} x_j = b,$$

where b is a constant. KKT system for this problem is

$$1 + v\prod_{\substack{i=1 \\ i \neq j}}^{n} x_i = 0 \quad \text{for } j = 1, ..., n$$

$$\prod_{j=1}^{n} x_j = b.$$

By multiplying the jth equation by x_j, $j = 1, ..., n$, and noting that $\prod\limits_{j=1}^{n} x_j = b$, we obtain

$$x_j + vb = 0 \quad \text{for } j = 1, ..., n.$$

Therefore, $\sum\limits_{j=1}^{n} x_j + nbv = 0$, which gives the unique value for the Lagrange multiplier $v = -\dfrac{1}{nb}$

$\sum\limits_{j=1}^{n} x_j$. By substituting this expression for v into each of the equations $x_j + vb = 0$ for $j = 1, ...,$

n, we then obtain $x_j = \dfrac{1}{n} \sum\limits_{k=1}^{n} x_j$ for $j = 1, ... , n$. This necessarily implies that values of x_j

must be identical, and since $\prod\limits_{j=1}^{n} x_j = b$, we have $\overline{x}_j = b^{1/n}$, $j = 1, ..., n$. Therefore, $\dfrac{1}{n} \sum\limits_{k=1}^{n} \overline{x}_j = $

$b^{1/n}$. We have thus shown that for any vector x such that $\prod\limits_{j=1}^{n} x_j = b$

$\dfrac{1}{n}\sum\limits_{j=1}^{n} x_j \geq \text{minimum } \{ \dfrac{1}{n}\sum\limits_{j=1}^{n} x_j : \prod\limits_{j=1}^{n} x_j = b \} = b^{1/n} = (\prod\limits_{j=1}^{n} x_j)^{1/n}.$

But, for any given vector x, the product of its coordinate is a constant, so that the above

inequality implies that $\dfrac{1}{n}\sum\limits_{j=1}^{n} x_j \geq (\prod\limits_{j=1}^{n} x_j)^{1/n}.$ $\qquad\square$

4.26. The KKT conditions for this problem are:

$$2(y_1 - y_{10})u_0 - u_1 + v = -1$$

$$2(y_i - y_{i0})u_0 - u_i + v = 0 \quad \text{for } i = 2, ..., n$$

$$\|y - y_0\|^2 \leq 1/n(n-1)$$

$$e^t y = 1$$

$$y \geq 0, \ u_0 \geq 0, \ u \geq 0, \ u_0(\|y - y_0\|^2 - 1/n(n-1)) = 0, \ u^t y = 0.$$

Let $\bar{y} = [0 \ \ \frac{1}{n-1} \ \ .... \ \ \frac{1}{n-1}]^t$. To show that $\bar{y}$ is a KKT point for this problem, all that one needs to do is substitute $\bar{y}$ for y in the foregoing KKT system and verify that the resulting system has a solution in u_0, u, and v. Readily, $\bar{y} \geq 0$, $e^t\bar{y} = (n-1)\frac{1}{n-1} = 1$, and $\bar{y} - y_0$ has $n-1$ coordinates equal to $\frac{1}{n(n-1)}$, and one coordinate equal to $-\frac{1}{n}$, so that $\|\bar{y} - y_0\|^2 = \frac{1}{n(n-1)}$. This means that $\bar{y}$ is a feasible solution. Moreover, since $\bar{y}_i > 0$ for $i = 2, ..., n$, we necessarily have $u_i = 0$ for $i = 2$, ..., n. Then, equations 2 through n of the KKT system yield $v = -\frac{2u_0}{n(n-1)}$, which together with the first equation gives $u_0 = \frac{n-1}{2}(1 + u_1)$. Thus, for any nonnegative u_1, u_0 is also nonnegative. This shows that $\bar{y}$ is a KKT point for this problem. The objective function in this problem is bounded below by 0, and its value at $\bar{y}$ is zero, therefore, $\bar{y}$ is an optimal solution.

4.27. In problem (1) we have $\nabla f(x) = c + H(x)$, and $\nabla g(x) = A^t$. Therefore, the KKT system is

$$c + Hx + A^t u = 0 \tag{a}$$

$$Ax + y = b \tag{b}$$

$$u^t y = 0$$

$$x \geq 0, \ y \geq 0, \ u \geq 0.$$

Since matrix H is invertible, equation (1) yields $H^{-1}c + x + H^{-1}A^t u = 0$. By premultiplying this equation by A, we obtain $AH^{-1}c + Ax + AH^{-1}A^t u = 0$, which can be rewritten as

$$AH^{-1}c + b + Ax - b + AH^{-1}A^t u = 0. \tag{c}$$

Next note that from equation (b) we have $y = b - Ax$, so that equation (c) can be further rewritten as

$$h + Gu - y = 0, \ u^t y = 0, \ u \geq 0, \ y \geq 0.$$

In problem (2) we have $\nabla f(v) = h + Gv$, and $\nabla g(v) = -I$. The KKT system for this problem is

$$h + Gv - z = 0, \ v^t z = 0, \ v \geq 0, \ z \geq 0,$$

where z is the vector of Lagrange multipliers. By comparing the two systems, we conclude that u = v, and y = z, that is that Lagrange multipliers in problem (1) are decision variables in problem (2), while Lagrange multipliers in (2) are slack variables in problem (1).

4.28. Assume that $\nabla f(\overline{x}) \neq 0$. Let $c^t = -\nabla_B f(\overline{x})^t B^{-1} N + \nabla_N f(\overline{x})^t$. The considered direction finding problem is a linear problem in which the function $c^t d$ is to be minimized over the region $\{d: 0 \leq d_j \leq 1, \ j \in I\}$. It is easy to verify that $c^t \overline{d} \leq 0$. In fact, an optimal solution to this problem is: $\overline{d}_j = 0$ if $c_j \geq 0$, and $\overline{d}_j = 1$ if $c_j < 0$. To prove that $\overline{d}$ is an improving direction we show that $\nabla f(\overline{x})^t \overline{d} < 0$. $\nabla f(\overline{x})^t \overline{d} = [\nabla_B f(\overline{x})^t \quad \nabla_N f(\overline{x})^t] \begin{bmatrix} \overline{d}_B \\ \overline{d}_N \end{bmatrix} = (-\nabla_B f(\overline{x})^t B^{-1} N + \nabla_N f(\overline{x})^t) \overline{d} = c^t \overline{d}$.

Therefore, $c^t \overline{d} < 0$ implies $\nabla f(\overline{x})^t \overline{d} < 0$, which means that $\overline{d}$ is an improving direction at $\overline{x}$. Moreover, $\overline{d}$ is a feasible direction at $\overline{x}$. First, note that

$$A\overline{d} = [\ B \ \ N] \begin{bmatrix} -B^{-1} N \overline{d}_N \\ \overline{d}_N \end{bmatrix} = -N\overline{d} + N\overline{d} = 0, \text{ and therefore, } A(\overline{x} + \lambda \overline{d}) = b \text{ for all } \lambda \geq 0.$$

Moreover, $\overline{x} + \lambda \overline{d} = [B^{-1} b - B^{-1} N \overline{d}_N \quad \overline{d}_N]$, which implies that $\overline{x} + \lambda \overline{d} \geq 0$ for all $\lambda \geq 0$, and $B^{-1} b - \lambda B^{-1} N \overline{d}_N \geq 0$ for $0 \leq \lambda \leq \overline{\lambda}$. Thus, indeed $\overline{d}$ is a feasible direction at $\overline{x}$.

Suppose that $\overline{d} = 0$. Then $c \geq 0$. The KKT conditions can then be written in the following way:

$$\nabla_B f(\overline{x}) - u_B + B^t v = 0$$

$$\nabla_N f(\overline{x}) - u_N + N^t v = 0$$

$$u_B^t \overline{x}_B = 0, \ u_N^t \overline{x}_N = 0, \ u_B \geq 0, \ u_N \geq 0.$$

Let $\overline{u}_B = 0$, $\overline{u}_N^t = \nabla_N f(\overline{x})^t - \nabla_B f(\overline{x})^t B^{-1} N$, and let $\overline{v}^t = -\nabla_B f(\overline{x})^t B^{-1}$. Simple algebra shows that $(\ \overline{u}_B \ , \ \overline{u}_N \ , \overline{v} \ )$ solves the above system. Therefore, $\overline{x}$ is a KKT point. $\qquad \square$

4.29. a. See the proof of Lemma 10.5.3.

b. See the proof of Theorem 10.5.4.

c. Assume that $\nabla f(\overline{x}) \neq 0$, since otherwise the problem is trivial.

First note that if in the given problem the constraint $||d||^2 \leq 1$ is replaced with $||d||^2 = 1$, then $\hat{d}$ is still an optimal solution. Next, note that $||-\nabla f(\overline{x}) - d||^2 = 2\nabla f(\overline{x})^t d + ||\nabla f(\overline{x})||^2 + ||d||^2$. This implies that problem

$$\text{minimize } \{\nabla f(\overline{x})^t d : A_1 d = 0, ||d||^2 = 1\}$$

is equivalent to

$$\text{minimize } \{||-\nabla f(\overline{x}) - d||^2 : A_1 d = 0, ||d||^2 = 1\},$$

because $||\nabla f(\overline{x})||^2$ and $||d||^2$ are constant terms. Vector $\overline{d} = -P\nabla f(\overline{x})$ is the closest to $-\nabla f(\overline{x})$ out of all vectors in the nullspace of A_1, that is out of all vectors d such that $A_1 d = 0$. Vector $\hat{d}$ is the closest to $-\nabla f(\overline{x})$ out of all normalized vectors in the nullspace of A_1, that is out of all vectors d such that $A_1 d = 0$, $||d||^2 = 1$. Therefore, there exists a positive scalar λ such that $\overline{d} = \lambda \hat{d}$ □

d. If $A = -I_n$, then A_1 is an mxn submatrix of $-I_n$, where m is the number of variables that are equal to zero at the current solution $\overline{x}$. Then $A_1 A_1^t = I_m$, and $A_1^t A_1 = \begin{bmatrix} I_m & 0 \\ 0 & 0 \end{bmatrix}$. Therefore, $P = \begin{bmatrix} 0 & 0 \\ 0 & I_{n-m} \end{bmatrix}$, and $\overline{d}_j = 0$ if $\overline{x}_j = 0$, and $\overline{d}_j = -\frac{\partial f(\overline{x})}{\partial x_j}$ if $\overline{x}_j > 0$.

4.31. Note that $C = \{d: Ad = 0\}$ is the nullspace of A, and P is the projection matrix onto the nullspace of A. If $d \in C$, then $Pd = d$. Also, for any $w \in E_n$ we have $Pw \in C$ by definition of matrix P and vector space C. This shows that $d \in C$ if and only if there exists $w \in E_n$ such that $Pw = d$. Next we show that if H is a symmetric matrix, then $d^t Hd \geq 0$ for any $d \in C$ if and only if $P^t HP$ is positive semidefinite.

($\Rightarrow$) Suppose that $d^t Hd \geq 0$ for any $d \in C$. Then, since for each $w \in E_n$ there exists $d \in C$ such that $Pw = d$, we obtain $w^t P^t HPw \geq 0$ for any $w \in E_n$. That is, matrix $P^t HP$ is positive semidefinite.

($\Leftarrow$) If $w^t P^t HPw \geq 0$ for any $w \in E_n$, then in particular for any $d \in C$ we have $d^t P^t HPd \geq 0$, which gives $d^t Hd \geq 0$ since for any $d \in C$ we have $Pd = d$. □

ANSWERS TO SELECTED EXERCISES

IN CHAPTER 5

5.3. Let T denote the cone of tangents of S at $\overline{x}$ as it is given in Definition 5.1.1.

a. Let W denote the set of directions defined in this part of exercise. That is, $d \in W$ if there exists a nonzero sequence $\{\beta_k\}$ convergent to zero, and a function $\alpha : E^1 \to E^n$ that converges to 0 as $\beta \to 0$, such that $\overline{x} + \beta_k d + \beta_k \alpha(\beta_k) \in S$ for any k. We need to show that $W = T$.

First, note that $0 \in W$, and $0 \in T$.

Let d be a nonzero vector from the set T. Then there exist a positive sequence $\{\lambda_k\}$ and a sequence $\{x_k\}$ of points from S convergent to $\overline{x}$ such that $d = \lim_{k \to \infty} \lambda_k(x_k - \overline{x})$. Therefore, for this sequence $\{x_k\}$ there exists a nonzero sequence $\{\beta_k\} \to 0$, for example one can take β_k such that $\beta_k d$ is the projection vector of $x_k - \overline{x}$ on vector d. Moreover, since $x_k \to \overline{x}$, there necessarily exists a function $\alpha : E^1 \to E^n$ convergent to 0 as $\beta \to 0$, such that $x_k = \overline{x} + \beta_k d + \beta_k \alpha(\beta_k)$. Therefore, $d \in W$.

Next, we show that if $d \in W$, then $d \in T$. For this purpose, let us note that if $d \in W$, then the sequence $\{x_k\}$, where $x_k = \overline{x} + \beta_k d + \beta_k \alpha(\beta_k)$, converges to $\overline{x}$, and moreover, the sequence $\{\frac{1}{\beta_k}(x_k - \overline{x}) - d\}$ converges to the zero vector. This shows that there exists a sequence $\{\lambda_k\}$, where $\lambda_k = \frac{1}{\beta_k}$, and a sequence $\{x_k\}$ of points from S convergent to $\overline{x}$ such that $d = \lim_{k \to \infty} \lambda_k(x_k - \overline{x})$. This means that $d \in T$, and thus completes the proof.

b. Again, let W denote the set of directions defined in this part of exercise. That is, $d \in W$ if there exists a nonnegative scalar λ and a sequence $\{x_k\}$ of points from S convergent to $\overline{x}$, $x_k \neq \overline{x}$, such that $d = \lim_{k \to \infty} \lambda \frac{x_k - \overline{x}}{\|x_k - \overline{x}\|}$. Also in this case, we have $0 \in W$ and $0 \in T$.

Let d be a nonzero vector in T. Then there exists a sequence $\{x_k\}$ of points from S different from $\overline{x}$ and a positive sequence $\{\lambda_k\}$ such that $x_k \to \overline{x}$, and $d = \lim_{k \to \infty} \lambda_k \|x_k - \overline{x}\| \frac{x_k - \overline{x}}{\|x_k - \overline{x}\|}$. Under the assumption that $d \in T$, the sequence $\{\lambda_k \|x_k - \overline{x}\|\}$ converges and $\lim\limits_{k \to \infty} \lambda_k \|x_k - \overline{x}\| = \|d\|$. Furthermore, the sequence $\left\{ \dfrac{x_k - \overline{x}}{\|x_k - \overline{x}\|} \right\}$ is contained in a compact set. Therefore, it must have a convergent subsequence. Without loss of generality, assume that the sequence $\left\{ \dfrac{x_k - \overline{x}}{\|x_k - \overline{x}\|} \right\}$ itself is convergent. If so, then we conclude that $d = \lim\limits_{k \to \infty} \lambda \dfrac{x_k - \overline{x}}{\|x_k - \overline{x}\|}$, where $\lambda = \|d\|$. Hence, $d \in W$. Finally, to show that $d \in T$ if $d \in W$, simply take $\lambda_k = \dfrac{\lambda}{\|x_k - \overline{x}\|} > 0$. This completes the proof. $\quad\square$

5.6. X is an open set, functions of nonbinding constraints are continuous at $\overline{x}$, and functions whose indices are in the set J are pseudoconcave. Therefore, by the same arguments as those used in the proof of Lemma 4.2.4, any vector d that satisfies inequalities $\nabla g_i(\overline{x})^t d \leq 0$ for $i \in J$, and $\nabla g_i(\overline{x})^t d < 0$ for $i \in I - J$ is a feasible direction at $\overline{x}$. If $\overline{x}$ is a local minimum, then the following system

$$\nabla f(\overline{x})^t d < 0$$

$$\nabla g_i(\overline{x})^t d < 0 \text{ for } i \in I - J$$

$$\nabla g_i(\overline{x})^t d \leq 0 \text{ for } i \in J$$

has no solution. By Motzkin's theorem of the alternative, we then conclude that there exists a nonzero solution to the system:

$$u_o \nabla f(x) + \sum_{i \in I\text{-}J} u_i \nabla g_i(\overline{x}) = 0,$$
$$u_0 \geq 0, \ u_i \geq 0 \text{ for } i \in I - J.$$

If $J = I$, then u_0 must be positive. Hence, suppose that $u_0 = 0$ and $I \neq J$. Then we have $\sum\limits_{i \in I\text{-}J} u_i \nabla g_i(\overline{x}) = 0$, where $u_i > 0$ for at least one $i \in I - J$. By taking the inner product of this equation and a vector d for which $\nabla g_i(\overline{x})^t d < 0$ (by assumption, at least one such vector exists), we obtain $\sum\limits_{i \in I\text{-}J} u_i \nabla g_i(\overline{x})^t d = 0$. However, since $u_i > 0$ for at least one $i \in I - J$, and $\nabla g_i(\overline{x})^t d < 0$ for all $i \in I - J$, we necessarily have $\sum\limits_{i \in I\text{-}J} u_i \nabla g_i(\overline{x})^t d < 0$. Thus a contradiction results. Therefore, $u_0 > 0$, and we can assert that $\overline{x}$ is a KKT point for this problem. $\quad\square$

5.7. a. See the proof of Theorem 10.1.7.

b. By part (a), $\bar{x}$ is a FJ point. Therefore, there exist nonzero scalars u_1, u_i, $i \in I$ such that

$$u_o \nabla f(\bar{x}) + \sum_{i \in I} u_i \nabla g_i(\bar{x}) = 0,$$
$$u_0 \geq 0, \ u_i \geq 0 \text{ for } i \in I.$$

If $u_0 = 0$, then the system

$$\sum_{i \in I} u_i \nabla g_i(\bar{x}) = 0,$$
$$u_i \geq 0 \text{ for } i \in I$$

has a nonzero solution. Then, by Gordan's Theorem, no vector d exists such that $\nabla g_i(\bar{x})^t d < 0$

for all $i \in I$. This means that $G_1 = \emptyset$, which contradicts the assumed constraint qualification (see

Exercise 5.5 d.).

5.10. a. $\bar{x} = [\ 1 \quad 0\ ]^t$, $I = \{1, 2\}$, $\nabla g_1(x) = [\ 2 \quad 0]^t$, $\nabla g_2(x) = [0 \ -1]^t$. Gradients of binding constraints

are linearly independent, hence, linear independence constraint qualification holds. This implies

that Kuhn-Tucker's constraint qualification holds (also, see comments following various

constraint qualifications in section 5.2).

b. If $\bar{x} = [1 \quad 0]$, then KKT equations

$$-1 \quad + 2u_1 \qquad = 0$$
$$u_2 \qquad = 0$$

yield the unique solution $u_1 = \frac{1}{2}$, $u_2 = 0$. Since Lagrange multipliers are nonnegative, and one of

them is positive, we conclude that $\bar{x}$ is a KKT point.

Note that a feasible solution must be in the unit circle centered at the origin, hence no feasible

solution can have its first coordinate greater than 1. Therefore, $\bar{x}$ is the global optimal solution.

5.15. We need to show that $G_1 \subseteq T$. Let d be a nonzero vector from G_1. If $\bar{d}^t d < 0$, then we readily have

$d \in D$, and hence, $d \in T$. (See the proof of Lemma 4.2.4 for details.) If $\bar{d}^t d = 0$, then there

necessarily exists a sequence $\{d_k\}$ of feasible points, such that $d_k \rightarrow \bar{d}$, $d_k \neq \bar{d}$, and $d_k^t d_k = 1$ so

that $d = \lim_{k \rightarrow \infty} \dfrac{d_k - \bar{d}}{||d_k - \bar{d}||}$. Therefore, $d \in T$.

ANSWERS TO SELECTED EXERCISES

IN CHAPTER 6

6.2. For simplicity, switch to minimization of $f(x) = -2x_1 - 3x_2 - x_3$.

a. $\theta(u) = \min\{(-2+u_1)x_1 + (-3 + u_1)x_2 + (-1 + u_2)x_3 : x \in X\} - 4u_1 - 2u_2$.

Set X has three extreme points $x_1 = (0, 0, 0)$, $x_2 = (1, 0, 0)$, and $x_3 = (0, 1, 0)$, and three extreme directions $d_1 = (0, 0, 1)$, $d_2 = (1, 0, 1)$, and $d_3 = (0, 1, 1)$. By examining the objective function at extreme points and along extreme directions we obtain the following expression for the dual function $\theta(u)$:

$$\theta(u) = \begin{cases} -4u_1 - 2u_2 & \text{if } u_1 \geq 3 \text{ and } u_2 \geq 1 \\ -3u_1 - 2u_2 - 3 & \text{if } u_1 + u_2 \geq 4 \text{ and } u_1 \leq 3 \\ -\infty & \text{otherwise.} \end{cases}$$

b. $\theta(u) = \min\{(-2+u_1)x_1 + (-3 + u_1)x_2 + (-1 - u_1 + u_2)x_3 : x \in X\} - u_1 - 2u_2 =$

$= \min\{(-2+u_1)x_1 + (-3 + u_1)x_2 : x_1 + x_2 \leq 4, x_1 \geq 0, x_2 \geq 0\}$

$+ \min\{(-1 - u_1 + u_2)x_3 : x_3 \geq 0\} - u_1 - 2u_2 =$

$$\theta(u) = \begin{cases} 3u_1 - 2u_2 - 12 & \text{if } -u_1 + u_2 \geq 1 \text{ and } u_1 \leq 3 \\ -u_1 - 2u_2 & \text{if } -u_1 + u_2 \geq 1 \text{ and } u_1 \geq 3 \\ -\infty & \text{otherwise.} \end{cases}$$

c. If possible, select those constraints to define X that will allow one to decompose the minimization problem into a finite number of independent problems.

6.4. Let $\theta_1(v_0, v)$ be the Lagrangian dual function for the transformed problem. That is,

$\theta_1(v_0, v) = \inf\{ f(x) + v_0^t(g(x) + s) + v^t h(x) : (x, s) \in X'\}$.

From the above formulation it follows that variables x and s can be separated, so that

$\theta_1(v_0, v) = \inf\{ f(x) + v_0^t g(x) + v^t h(x): x \in X \} + \inf\{ v_0^t s: s \geq 0 \}.$

Note that if $v_0 \geq 0$, then $\inf\{ v_0^t s: s \geq 0 \} = 0$, and otherwise $\inf\{ v_0^t s: s \geq 0 \} = -\infty$.

Therefore, the dual problem seeks unconstrained maximum of $\theta_1(v_0, v)$, where

$$\theta_1(v_0, v) = \begin{cases} \inf \{ f(x) + v_0^t g(x) + v^t h(x): x \in X \} & \text{if } v_0 \geq 0 \\ \\ -\infty & \text{otherwise.} \end{cases}$$

This representation of $\theta_1(v_0, v)$ shows that the two dual problems are equivalent ($v_0 = u$).

6.7. Let $y_\lambda = \lambda y_1 + (1-\lambda)y_2$, where $\lambda \in (0,1)$. We need to show that $\nu(y_\lambda) \leq \lambda\nu(y_1)+(1-\lambda)\nu(y_2)$. For this purpose, let

$X(y_1) = \{x : g_i(x) \leq y_{i1}, i = 1, ..., m, h_i(x) = y_{m+i,1}, i = 1, ..., \ell, x \in X \}$

$X(y_2) = \{x : g_i(x) \leq y_{i2}, i = 1, ..., m, h_i(x) = y_{m+i,2}, i = 1, ..., \ell, x \in X \}$

$X(y_\lambda) = \{x : g_i(x) \leq y_{i\lambda}, i = 1, ..., m, h_i(x) = y_{m+i,\lambda}, i = 1, ..., \ell, x \in X \}$

$\nu(y_k) = f(x_k), k = 1, 2,$ and let

$\nu(y_\lambda) = f(x^*).$

By definition of the perturbation function $\nu(y)$ this means that

$x_k \in X(y_k)$ and $f(x_k) = \min\{f(x): x \in X(y_k)\}, k = 1, 2$ and

$x^* \in X(y_\lambda)$ and $f(x^*) = \min\{f(x): x \in X(y_\lambda)\}$

Under the given assumptions (functions $g_i(x)$ are convex, functions $h_i(x)$ are affine, and set X is convex) we have $x_\lambda = \lambda x_1 + (1-\lambda)x_2 \in X(y_\lambda)$ for any $\lambda \in [0, 1]$. But $f(x^*) = \min\{f(x): x \in X(y_\lambda)\}$, therefore, we have $f(x^*) \leq f(x_\lambda)$, which together with convexity of $f(x)$ implies that $\nu(y_\lambda) = f(x^*) \leq \lambda f(x_1)+(1-\lambda)f(x_2) = \lambda\nu(y_1) + (1-\lambda)\nu(y_2)$. This completes the proof. $\square$

6.10. Let $\gamma = \inf\{ f(x) : g(x) \leq 0, h(x) = 0, x \in X\}$. Readily, γ is a finite number, since $\bar{x}$ solves problem P: minimize $f(x)$ subject to $g(x) \leq 0, h(x) = 0, x \in X$. Moreover, the system

$f(x) - \gamma < 0, \quad g(x) \leq 0, \quad h(x) = 0, \quad x \in X$

has no solution. By Lemma 6.2.3, it then follows that there exists a nonzero vector $(\bar{u}_0, \bar{u}, \bar{v})$, such that $(\overline{u}_0, \overline{u}) \geq 0$, and $\overline{u}_0(f(x) - \gamma) + \overline{u}^t g(x) + \overline{v}^t h(x) \geq 0$ for all $x \in X$. That is,

$\phi(\overline{u}_0, \overline{u}, \overline{v}, x) \geq \overline{u}_0 \gamma$ for all $x \in X$. But, since $\overline{x}$ solves problem P, in fact we have $\gamma = f(\overline{x})$.

Moreover, $h(\overline{x}) = 0$ and $g(\overline{x}) \leq 0$, so that $\overline{v}^t h(x) = 0$, and $\overline{u}^t g(\overline{x}) \leq 0$. Therefore, for any x in X

$$\phi(\overline{u}_0, \overline{u}, \overline{v}, x) \geq \overline{u}_0 f(\overline{x}) + \overline{u}^t g(\overline{x}) + \overline{v}^t h(\overline{x}) = \phi(\overline{u}_0, \overline{u}, \overline{v}, \overline{x}).$$

To prove the other inequality, note that

$\phi(\overline{u}_0, \overline{u}, \overline{v}, \overline{x}) - \phi(\overline{u}_0, u, v, \overline{x}) = (\overline{u} - u)^t g(\overline{x}) + (\overline{v} - v)^t h(\overline{x}) = (\overline{u} - u)^t g(\overline{x}) \geq \overline{u}^t g(\overline{x}).$

If $\overline{u}_0 > 0$, then $\overline{u}^t g(\overline{x}) = 0$ as shows in the proof of Theorem 6.2.4, . If $\overline{u}_0 = 0$, then we have

$\phi(\overline{u}_0, \overline{u}, \overline{v}, \overline{x}) \geq 0$, that is, $\overline{u}^t g(\overline{x}) + \overline{v}^t h(\overline{x}) \geq 0$. But $g(\overline{x}) \leq 0$ since $\overline{x}$ is a feasible solution, and

$\overline{u} \geq 0$, therefore, we necessarily obtain $\overline{u}^t g(\overline{x}) = 0$. This implies that for any $u \geq 0$

$\phi(\overline{u}_0, \overline{u}, \overline{v}, \overline{x}) - \phi(\overline{u}_0, u, v, \overline{x}) \geq 0.$ $\square$

6.15. For any linear function f(x) we have min $\{f(x): Dx = d, x \in X\} = $ min $\{f(x): x \in H[x \in X : Dx = d]\}$.

Therefore, for each fixed π

$\theta(\pi) = $ min $\{c^t x + \pi^t (Ax - b) : Dx = d, x \in X\} = $ min $\{c^t x + \pi^t (Ax - b) : x \in H[x \in X : Dx = d]\}.$

Moreover, by the strong duality theorem

max $\theta(\pi) = $ min $\{c^t x : Ax = b, x \in H[x \in X : Dx = d]\}.$

Note that $\{x: Ax = b, Dx = d, x \in X\} \subset \{x: Ax = b, x \in H[x \in X : Dx = d]\}$, therefore,

min $\{c^t x: Ax = b, Dx = d, x \in X\} \geq $ min$\{c^t x: Ax = b, x \in H[x \in X : Dx = d]\}$, which implies that

min $\{c^t x: Ax = b, Dx = d, x \in X\} \geq $ max $\theta(\pi)$. $\square$

6.17 a. $\theta(u) = $ min$\{-2x_1 + 2x_2 + x_3 - 3x_4 + u_1(x_1 + x_2 + x_3 + x_4 - 8) + u_2(x_1 - 2x_3 + 4x_4 - 2) : x \in X\} = $

min$\{(-2 + u_1 + u_2)x_1 + (2 + u_1)x_2 : x_1 + x_2 \leq 8, x_1 \geq 0, x_2 \geq 0\} + $

min$\{(1 + u_1 - 2u_2)x_3 + (-3 + u_1 + 4u_2)x_4 : x_3 + 2x_4 \leq 6, x_3 \geq 0, x_4 \geq 0)\} - 8u_1 - 2u_2.$

$\theta(u) = \theta_i(u)$ if $u \in U_i$, i = 1, ..., 7, where

$\theta_1(u) = 22 + 6u_1 - 14u_2$ and $U_1 = \{(u_1, u_2): u_1 \leq -2, u_2 \geq 4\}$

$\theta_2(u) = 6 - 2u_1 - 14u_2$ and $U_2 = \{(u_1, u_2): u_1 \geq -2, u_1 + u_2 \geq 2, u_1 - 2u_2 \leq -1\}$

$\theta_3(u) = -8u_1 - 2u_2$ and $U_3 = \{(u_1, u_2): u_1 - 2u_2 \geq -1, u_1 + u_2 \geq 2, u_1 + 4u_2 \geq 3\}$

$\theta_4(u) = -9 - 5u_1 + 10u_2$ and $U_4 = \{(u_1, u_2): u_1 + 4u_2 \leq 3, u_1 + u_2 \geq 2\}$

$\theta_5(u) = -16 + 6u_2$ and $U_5 = \{(u_1, u_2): u_1 - 2u_2 \geq -1, u_1 + u_2 \leq 2, u_1 + 4u_2 \geq 3\}$

$\theta_6(u) = -25 + 3u_1 + 18u_2$ and $U_6 = \{(u_1, u_2): -u_1 + 8u_2 \leq 5, u_1 + 4u_2 \leq 3, u_1 + u_2 \leq 2\}$

$\theta_7(u) = -10 + 6u_1 - 6u_2$ and $U_7 = \{(u_1, u_2): u_2 \leq 4, u_1 + u_2 \leq 2, u_1 - 2u_2 \leq -1, -u_1 + 8u_2 \geq 5\}$

b. $u = (4, 0) \in U_3$, therefore $\nabla\theta(4, 0) = (-8, -2)$.

c. The second coordinate of $(4, 0) + \lambda(-8, -2)$ is -2λ, which is nonpositive for all $\lambda \geq 0$.

Therefore, the gradient of $\theta(u)$ at $(4, 0)$ is not a feasible direction at $(4, 0)$.

$d = (-8, 0)$ is a feasible direction of $\theta(u)$ at $(4, 0)$.

d. To maintain feasibility, λ is restricted to values in the interval $[0, 1/2]$ only.

$\theta((4, 0) + \lambda(-8, 0)) = \theta((4 - 8\lambda, 0)) =$

$= \text{minimum}\{(2 - 8\lambda)x_1 + (6 - 8\lambda)x_2: x_1 + x_2 \leq 8, x_1 \geq 0, x_2 \geq 0\} +$

$\quad \text{minimum}\{(5 - 8\lambda)x_3 + (1 - 8\lambda)x_4: x_3 + 2x_4 \leq 6, x_3 \geq 0, x_4 \geq\} - 32(1 - 2\lambda) =$

$\quad\quad -32 + 64\lambda \quad\quad \text{for } 0 \leq \lambda < 1/8$

$\quad\quad -29 + 40\lambda \quad\quad \text{for } 1/8 \leq \lambda < 1/4$

$\quad\quad -13 - 24\lambda \quad\quad \text{for } 1/4 \leq \lambda \leq 1/2.$

Maximum of $\theta((4 - 8\lambda, 0))$ over the interval $[0, 1/2]$ is -19, and is attained at $\lambda = 1/4$.

6.18. First we show that if $(d_u, d_v) = (0, 0)$, then $(\overline{u}, \overline{v})$ solves problem (D).

Problem (D) seeks maximum of a concave function over $\{(u, v): u \geq 0\}$, therefore, the KKT conditions are both necessary and sufficient for optimality. To show that $(\overline{u}, \overline{v})$ is a KKT point for (D), we need to demonstrate that there exists a vector (z_1, z_2) such that

$$-\nabla_u\theta(\overline{u}, \overline{v})^t - \nabla_v\theta(\overline{u}, \overline{v})^t - z_1 = 0$$

$$z_1^t\overline{u} = 0, z_1 \geq 0.$$

By assumption, we have $\nabla_v\theta(\overline{u}, \overline{v}) = h(\overline{x}) = 0$, and $\nabla_u\theta(\overline{u}, \overline{v}) = g(\overline{x})$. Moreover, since $d_u = 0$, we necessarily have $g(\overline{x}) \leq 0$ and $g(\overline{x})^t\overline{u} = 0$. Thus $z_1 = g(\overline{x})$ solves the KKT system, which implies that $(\bar{u},\bar{v})$ solves (D).

Next we need to show that if $(d_u, d_v) \neq (0, 0)$, then (d_u, d_v) is a feasible and ascent direction of $\theta(u,v)$ at $(\bar{u},\bar{v})$. Notice that v is a vector of unrestricted variables, and by construction, $d_{i_u} \geq 0$ whenever $\bar{u}_i = 0$, therefore, (d_u, d_v) is a feasible direction at $(\bar{u},\bar{v})$. To show that it is also an ascent direction, let us consider $\nabla\theta(\bar{u},\bar{v})^t d$:

$$\nabla\theta(\bar{u},\bar{v})^t d = \nabla_u\theta(\bar{u},\bar{v})^t d_u + \nabla_v\theta(\bar{u},\bar{v})^t d_v = g(\bar{x})^t g(\bar{x}) + h(\bar{x})^t h(\bar{x})$$

$$= h(\bar{x})^t h(\bar{x}) + \sum_{\bar{u}_i > 0} g_i^2(\bar{x}) + \sum_{\bar{u}_i = 0} g_i(\bar{x})\max(0, g_i(\bar{x})).$$

At least one of the functions $g_i(x)$, $i = 1, ..., m$ and $h_{m+i}(x)$, $i = 1, ..., \ell$ takes on a positive value at $\bar{x}$ (otherwise, $(d_u, d_v)=(0, 0)$), therefore, $h(\bar{x})^t h(\bar{x}) + \sum_{\bar{u}_i > 0} g_i^2(\bar{x}) + \sum_{\bar{u}_i = 0} g_i(\bar{x})\max(0, g_i(\bar{x}))>0$, and thus $\nabla\theta(\bar{u},\bar{v})^t d > 0$. This demonstrates that (d_u, d_v) is an ascent direction of $\theta(u,v)$ at $(\bar{u},\bar{v})$. $\square$

In the given numerical example, $\theta(u_1,u_2) = \min \{x_1^2 + x_2^2 + u_1(-x_1-x_2+4) + u_2(x_1+ 2x_2- 8): (x_1, x_2)\in E_2\}$.

Iteration 1. $(u_1, u_2) = (0, 0)$.

At $(u_1, u_2) = (0, 0)$ we have $\theta(0,0) = 0$, and $\bar{x}_1 = \bar{x}_2 = 0$. Thus, $d_1 = \max(0, 4) = 4$, and $d_2 = \max (0,-8) = 0$. Next, we need to find maximum of function $\theta(u_1,u_2)$ along direction $(4, 0)$. Notice that $\theta((0,0) + \lambda(4,0)) = \theta(4\lambda,0) = \min\{ x_1^2 + x_2^2 + 4\lambda(-x_1 - x_2 + 4): (x_1, x_2)\in E_2\} =$

$= \min\{ x_1^2 - 4\lambda x_1: x_1\in E\} +\min\{ x_2^2 - 4\lambda x_2: x_2\in E\} + 16\lambda = -8\lambda^2 + 16\lambda$, and

$\text{maximum}\{\theta(4\lambda,0): \lambda \geq 0\} = \theta(4,0)$, that is $\lambda^* = 1$.

Iteration 2. $(u_1, u_2) = (4,0)$.

At $(u_1, u_2) = (4, 0)$ we have $\theta(4,0) = \min \{x_1^2 + x_2^2 + 4(-x_1 - x_2 + 4): (x_1, x_2)\in E_2\} = 8$, and $\bar{x}_1 = \bar{x}_2 = 2$. Then $d_1 = g_1(2,2) =0$, and $d_2 = \max(0, -2) = 0$. Based on the property of the dual problem, we conclude that at $(u_1,u_2) = (4,0)$ the Lagrangian dual function $\theta(u_1,u_2)$ attains its maximum value. Thus $(\bar{u}_1, \bar{u}_2) = (4,0)$ is the (unique) optimal solution to (D).

6.28. Assume that $X \neq \emptyset$.

a. The dual problem is: maximize $\theta(v)$, where $\theta(v) = \min\{ f(x) + v^t(Ax-b): x \in X\}$.

b. The proof of concavity of $\theta(v)$ is identical to that of Theorem 6.3.1.

   X is a nonempty compact polyhedral set, and for each fixed v, the function $f(x) + v^t(Ax-b)$ is concave, therefore, by Theorem 3.4.7 there exists an extreme point $\hat{x}$ of X such that $\theta(v) = f(\hat{x}) + \hat{v}^t(A\hat{x}-b)$. Moreover, since the number of extreme points of X is finite, the dual function $\theta(v)$ is composed of a finite number of linear functions.

c. For a given $\hat{v}$, let $X(\hat{v})$ denote the set of optimal solutions to the problem of minimization of $f(x) + v^t(Ax-b)$ over X. Then, by Theorem 6.3.7, $\xi(\hat{v})$ is a subgradient of $\theta(v)$ at $\hat{v}$ if and only if $\xi(\hat{v}) = Ax-b$ for some x in the convex hull of $X(\hat{v})$.

   Vector d is an ascent direction of $\theta(v)$ at $\hat{v}$ if $(Ax-b)^t d > 0$ for some x in the convex hull of $X(\hat{v})$. If $Ax = b$ for some $x \in X(\hat{v})$, then the set of ascent directions of $\theta(v)$ at v is empty. Otherwise, an ascent direction exists. In this case, the steepest ascent direction, $\hat{d}$, can be found by employing Theorem 6.3.11. Namely, $\hat{d} = \hat{\xi}/\|\hat{\xi}\|$, where $\hat{\xi}$ is a subgradient of $\theta(v)$ at $\hat{v}$ with the smallest Euclidean norm. To find $\hat{\xi}$ one needs to solve the following problem: minimize $\|Ax-b\|$ subject to $x \in H[X(\hat{v})]$. If $\hat{x}$ is an optimal solution for this problem, then $\hat{\xi} = A\hat{x} - b$.

d. If X is not bounded, then it is not necessarily true that for each v there exists an optimal solution for the problem minimize $f(x) + v^t(Ax-b)$ subject to $x \in X$. For all such vectors the dual function $\theta(v)$ is simply not defined. However, $\theta(v)$ is still concave and piecewise linear over the set of all vectors v, for which $\min\{ f(x) + v^t(Ax-b): x \in X\}$ exists.

ANSWERS TO SELECTED EXERCISES

IN CHAPTER 7

7.5. It needs to be shown that for any sequences $\{x_k\}$ and $\{v_k\}$, if

     1. $x_k \in X$, $x_k \to \overline{x}$,

     2. $v_k \in C(x_k)$, $v_k \to \overline{v}$,

then $\overline{v} \in C(\overline{x})$. By definition of mapping C, $v \in C(x)$ means that there exist vectors $a \in A(x)$ and $b \in B(x)$ such that $v = a + b$. Hence, what needs to be shown is that under the given assumptions, we have $\overline{v} = \overline{a} + \overline{b}$, where $\overline{a} \in A(\overline{x})$, and $\overline{b} \in B(\overline{x})$. For this purpose see the answer to Exercise 2.9.

7.6. We show that for any sequence $\{x_n, z_n\} \to (\overline{x}, \overline{z})$, if $\{y_n\} \to \overline{y}$, where $y_n \in A(x_n, z_n)$ for each n, then $\overline{y} \in A(\overline{x}, \overline{z})$. The proof below is general in the sense that it does not use any specific vector norm.

By definition of y_n, we have

$$y_n = \lambda_n x_n + (1-\lambda_n)z_n, \text{ where } \lambda_n \in [0, 1] \text{ is such that}$$

$$\|y_n\| \le \|\lambda x_n + (1-\lambda)z_n\| \text{ for any } \lambda \in [0, 1].$$

Note that sequence $\{\lambda_n\}$ is bounded, hence it must have a convergent subsequence. For notational simplicity and without loss of generality, assume that the sequence $\{\lambda_n\}$ itself converges, and let $\overline{\lambda}$ denote its limit. Then we can directly evaluate the limit $\overline{y}$ of $\{y_n\}$, that is $\overline{y} = \overline{\lambda}\overline{x} + (1-\overline{\lambda})\overline{z}$. It remains to show that $\|\overline{y}\| \le \|\lambda\overline{x} + (1-\lambda)\overline{z}\|$ for any $\lambda \in [0, 1]$. For this purpose note that for each n we have

$$\|y_n\| \le \| \lambda(x_n-\overline{x}) + (1-\lambda)(z_n-\overline{z}) + \lambda\overline{x} + (1-\lambda)\overline{z}\| \text{ for any } \lambda \in [0, 1].$$

By properties of vector norm $\|.\|$, we next obtain that for each n

$||y_n|| \leq || \lambda(x_n - \overline{x})|| + ||(1-\lambda)(z_n - \overline{z})|| + || \lambda\overline{x} + (1-\lambda)\overline{z}||$ for any $\lambda \in [0, 1]$.

Finally, by taking the limit as $n \to \infty$ we obtain

$||\overline{y}|| \leq || \lambda\overline{x} + (1-\lambda)\overline{z}||$ for any $\lambda \in [0, 1]$, which completes the proof. $\square$

7.7. We need to show that for any sequence $\{x_n, z_n\} \to (\overline{x}, \overline{z})$, if $\{y_n\} \to \overline{y}$, where for each n,

$||y_n - x_n|| \leq z_n$ and $||y_n|| \leq ||w||$ for any w such that $||w - x_n|| \leq z_n$,

then $||\overline{y} - \overline{x}|| \leq \overline{z}$ and $||\overline{y}|| \leq ||w||$ for any w such that $||w - \overline{x}|| \leq \overline{z}$.

By contradiction, suppose that there exists a vector w_* such that $||w_* - \overline{x}|| \leq \overline{z}$, and $||w_*|| < ||\overline{y}||$. Then, there must exist N such that

$||w_* - x_n|| \leq z_n$ and $||w_*|| \leq ||y_n||$

whenever $n \geq N$. If $||w_*|| = ||y_n||$ for all $n \geq N$, then we have $||w_*|| = ||\overline{y}||$, thus a contradiction. If on the other hand, $||w_*|| < ||y_n||$ for some $n \geq N$, then again a contradiction results since $y_n \in A(x_n, z_n)$ for each n. $\square$

7.8. Let Y denote the set $\{y: By + b, y \geq 0\}$. We need to show that for any sequence $\{x_k\}$ convergent to $\overline{x}$, if for each k, y_k is an optimal solution to the problem: minimize $x_k^t y$ subject to $y \in Y$, and $\{y_k\} \to \overline{y}$, then $\overline{y}$ solves the problem: minimize $x^t y$ subject to $y \in Y$.

Note that for each k we have

$y_k \in Y$, and $x_k^t y_k \leq x_k^t y$ for all $y \in Y$.

As a result of taking the limit of this inequality as $k \to \infty$ we obtain $\overline{x}^t \overline{y} \leq \overline{x}^t y$ for all $y \in Y$. Set Y is closed, and therefore, for any convergent sequence of points from this set its limit is in Y. Hence, $\overline{y} \in Y$. $\square$

7.11. See the proof of Lemma 5.1, and comments that follow it in *Nonlinear Programming* by Willard I. Zangwill, Prentice Hall, Inc., Englewood Cliffs, N.J., 1969.

7.17. a. With $\alpha(x) = x^2$, and mapping C defined in the exercise, we have :

if $x \in [-1, 1]$, then $y = C(x) = x$, and hence, $\alpha(y) = \alpha(x)$

if $x < -1$, then $y = C(x) = x+1$, and hence, $\alpha(y) = (x+1)^2 < x^2 = \alpha(x)$

if $x > 1$, then $y = C(x) = x-1$, and hence, $\alpha(y) = (x-1)^2 < x^2 = \alpha(x)$.

Apparently, mapping B is closed over $(-\infty, 0) \cup (0, \infty)$, and moreover, if $x \neq 0$, and $y = B(x)$, then $y = \frac{x}{2}$, and hence $\alpha(y) = \frac{x^2}{4} < x^2 = \alpha(x)$. Thus, both mappings C and B, satisfy all the assumptions of Theorem 7.3.4

b. For any x we have $A(x) = C(B(x)) = C(\frac{x}{2})$, which by definition of mapping C means that mapping $A(x)$ is as given in part (b) of this exercise. It can be easily verified that the composite mapping A is not closed at $x = -2$ and at $x = 2$.

c. If the starting point $x_0 \in [-2, 2]$, then for each k we have $x_k \in [-2, 2]$, and thus $x_{k+1} = \frac{x_k}{2}$, which yields $\{x_k\} \rightarrow 0$.

If the starting point $x_0 < -2$, then there exists K such that if $k \leq K$, then $x_k < -2$, and if $k > K$, then $x_k \in [-2, 2]$. This means that except for a finite number of terms, all terms of the sequence $\{x_k\}$ are in the interval $[-2, 2]$, and thus $x_{k+1} = \frac{x_k}{2}$, and $\{x_k\} \rightarrow 0$.

Similar arguments can be used to show that if $x_0 > 2$, then still $\{x_k\} \rightarrow 0$.

ANSWERS TO SELECTED EXERCISES

IN CHAPTER 8

8.4. a. ($\Rightarrow$) Under the given assumptions we have

there exists $\overline{\lambda} \in$ [a, b] such that $\theta(\overline{\lambda}) \leq \theta(\lambda)$ for all $\lambda \in$[a, b], and

for any $\lambda_1, \lambda_2 \in$ [a, b] such that $\lambda_1 < \lambda_2$ 　　(1) if $\lambda_2 \leq \overline{\lambda}$ then $\theta(\lambda_1) > \theta(\lambda_2)$

　　　　　　　　　　　　　　　　　(2) if $\lambda_1 \geq \overline{\lambda}$ then $\theta(\lambda_1) < \theta(\lambda_2)$.

Let λ_1 and λ_2 be any two distinct numbers from the interval [a, b]. Without loss of generality assume that $\lambda_1 < \lambda_2$. Further, let $\hat{\lambda} \in (\lambda_1, \lambda_2)$. We need to show that $\theta(\hat{\lambda}) < \max \{\theta(\lambda_1), \theta(\lambda_2)\}$ for any $\hat{\lambda} \in (\lambda_1, \lambda_2)$.

If $\lambda_2 \leq \overline{\lambda}$, then by (1) we have $\max \{\theta(\lambda_1), \theta(\lambda_2)\} = \theta(\lambda_1)$. Moreover, (1) yields $\theta(\hat{\lambda}) < \theta(\lambda_1)$ because $\lambda_1 < \hat{\lambda} < \overline{\lambda}$. Therefore, $\theta(\hat{\lambda}) < \max \{\theta(\lambda_1), \theta(\lambda_2)\}$.

If $\lambda_1 \geq \overline{\lambda}$, then by (2) we have $\max \{\theta(\lambda_1), \theta(\lambda_2)\} = \theta(\lambda_2)$, and furthermore, by (2) again $\theta(\hat{\lambda}) < \theta(\lambda_2)$ because $\lambda_2 > \hat{\lambda} > \overline{\lambda}$.

Finally, if $\lambda_1 < \overline{\lambda} < \lambda_2$, then $\hat{\lambda}$ must be in the interval $(\lambda_1, \overline{\lambda}]$ or else in the interval $(\overline{\lambda}, \lambda_2)$. In the latter case we have $\theta(\hat{\lambda}) < \theta(\lambda_2) \leq \max \{\theta(\lambda_1), \theta(\lambda_2)\}$ by the assumption (2). In the former one, assumption (1) yields $\theta(\hat{\lambda}) < \theta(\lambda_1) \leq \max \{\theta(\lambda_1), \theta(\lambda_2)\}$.

Therefore, $\theta(\hat{\lambda}) < \max \{\theta(\lambda_1), \theta(\lambda_2)\}$ for any $\hat{\lambda} \in (\lambda_1, \lambda_2)$, which proves that $\theta(\lambda)$ is strongly quasiconvex over the interval [a, b].

($\Leftarrow$) Suppose that $\theta(\lambda)$ is strongly quasiconvex over the interval [a, b] and attains its minimum value over this interval at $\overline{\lambda}$. Note that the minimizer $\overline{\lambda}$ is necessarily unique. Consider any two values λ_1 and λ_2 from the interval [a, b] such that $\lambda_1 < \lambda_2$. If $\lambda_1 = \overline{\lambda}$ or $\lambda_2 = \overline{\lambda}$, then we readily have $\theta(\lambda_1) > \theta(\lambda_2)$ or $\theta(\lambda_2) > \theta(\lambda_1)$ respectively, because $\overline{\lambda}$ is the unique minimizer of $\theta(\lambda)$ over the interval [a, b]. If $\lambda_1 > \overline{\lambda}$, then $\lambda_1 \in (\overline{\lambda}, \lambda_2)$, and $\theta(\lambda_1) < \max \{ \theta(\overline{\lambda}), \theta(\lambda_2) \} = \theta(\lambda_2)$. The last inequality follows from the assumed strong quasiconvexity of $\theta(\lambda)$, and the equality follows from the assumption that $\bar{\lambda}$ minimizes $\theta(\lambda)$ over [a, b]. If $\lambda_2 < \bar{\lambda}$, then $\lambda_2 \in (\lambda_1, \bar{\lambda})$, and by similar arguments we obtain $\theta(\lambda_2) < \theta(\lambda_1)$. This completes the proof that $\theta(\lambda)$ is strongly unimodal over the interval [a, b]. $\square$

b. The proof follows basically the same arguments as in part a.

8.15. a. We need to show that if $\theta_1 = \theta_2 = \theta_3$, then $\theta_1 = \min\{\theta(\lambda): \lambda \geq 0\}$.

By contradiction, suppose $\min\{\theta(\lambda): \lambda \geq 0\} = \theta(\lambda^*) < \theta_1$. Then by strict quasiconvexity of $\theta(\lambda)$, since $\max\left(\theta(\lambda^*), \theta(\lambda_1)\right) = \max\left(\theta(\lambda^*), \theta(\lambda_2)\right) = \theta(\lambda_1) = \theta(\lambda_2)$, we obtain

$\theta(\lambda) < \theta_1$ for any λ between λ_1 and λ^* if $\lambda_1 < \lambda^*$, and

$\theta(\lambda) < \theta_2$ for any λ between λ_2 and λ^* if $\lambda_1 > \lambda^*$.

Thus in particular, we have $\theta(\lambda_2) < \theta(\lambda_1)$ in the former case, and $\theta(\lambda_1) < \theta(\lambda_2)$ in the latter one. Both cases are in contradiction with $\theta_1 = \theta_2$. Therefore, $\theta_1 = \min\{\theta(\lambda): \lambda \geq 0\}$. $\square$

b. Continuity of $\bar{\theta}(\lambda)$ follows directly from its definition ant continuity of $\theta(\lambda)$. Next, we need to show that $\bar{\theta}(\lambda_{new}) < \bar{\theta}(\lambda)$ whenever θ_1, θ_2, and θ_3 are not all equal to each other.

Minimizer $\bar{\lambda}$ of $\theta(\lambda)$ is in the interval (λ_1, λ_3). If $\bar{\lambda} > \lambda_2$, and $\bar{\theta} \geq \theta_2$, then

$\bar{\theta}(\lambda_{new}) = \bar{\theta}(\lambda) + \bar{\theta} - \theta_3 < \bar{\theta}(\lambda) + \theta_3 - \theta_3 = \bar{\theta}(\lambda)$.

If $\bar{\lambda} > \lambda_2$, and $\bar{\theta} \leq \theta_2$, then

$\bar{\theta}(\lambda_{new}) = \bar{\theta}(\lambda) + \bar{\theta} - \theta_1 < \bar{\theta}(\lambda) + \theta_1 - \theta_1 = \bar{\theta}(\lambda)$, since $\bar{\theta} \leq \theta_2 \leq \theta_1$.

Similar derivations lead to $\bar{\theta}(\lambda_{new}) < \bar{\theta}(\lambda)$ if $\bar{\lambda} < \lambda_2$, and if $\bar{\lambda} = \lambda_2$.

8.18. Let $y = K_k$, and let $g(y) = \dfrac{y^2\alpha(\alpha-1)^2}{(y^2+\alpha^3)(y^2+\alpha)}$. We need to show that the function g(y) attains its maximum at y such that $y^2 = \alpha^2$. To establish this result note that

$g'(y) = \dfrac{2y\alpha(\alpha-1)^2}{[(y^2+\alpha^3)(y^2+\alpha)]^2} (\alpha^4 - y^4)$. It can be now easily verified using basic calculus that

maximum of g(y) occurs at $y^2 = \alpha^2$, which completes the proof. $\square$

8.19. First, let us prove Kantorovich inequality. Matrix H is assumed to be symmetric and positive definite, therefore there exist matrices Q and D, where Q is orthogonal and D is diagonal, with positive diagonal entries, such that $H = QDQ^t$. Diagonal entries d_i, $i = 1,\dots,n$ of matrix D are simply eigenvalues of matrix H. This allows us to assert that

$$\min_{x \neq 0} \frac{x^t x}{(x^t H x)(x^t H^{-1} x)} = \min_{x \neq 0} \frac{x^t x}{(x^t D x)(x^t D^{-1} x)} = \min_{||x||=1} \frac{1}{(x^t D x)(x^t D^{-1} x)} \cdot$$

For any normalized vector x the expression $x^t D x$ is simply a convex combination of d_1, d_2, ..., d_n, that is it represents some value from the interval $[d_1, d_n]$, where d_1, d_n are the smallest and the largest eigenvalues of H. Therefore, for any fixed x there exists a unique $\beta \in [0, 1]$ such that $x^t D x = \beta d_1 + (1-\beta) d_n$. Simultaneously, the expression $x^t D^{-1} x$ is a convex combination of reciprocals of d_1, d_2, ..., d_n, and therefore, if $x^t D x = \beta d_1 + (1-\beta) d_n$, where $0 \leq \beta \leq 1$, then $x^t D^{-1} x \leq \beta \frac{1}{d_1} + (1-\beta) \frac{1}{d_n}$. This yields

$$\min_{||x||=1} \frac{1}{(x^t D x)(x^t D^{-1} x)} \geq \min \{[\beta d_1 + (1-\beta) d_n]^{-1} [\beta \frac{1}{d_1} + (1-\beta) \frac{1}{d_n}]^{-1} : 0 \leq \beta \leq 1\}.$$

From simple calculus it then follows that the expression on the left hand side of the last inequality is minimized at $\beta = \frac{1}{2}$. Therefore,

$$\min \{[\beta d_1 + (1-\beta) d_n]^{-1} [\beta \frac{1}{d_1} + (1-\beta) \frac{1}{d_n}]^{-1} : 0 \leq \beta \leq 1\} = [(d_1 + d_n)^2 / (4 d_1 d_n)]^{-1} =$$

$$= 4\alpha / (1 + \alpha^2),$$ where $\alpha = d_n / d_1$. This completes the proof of Kantorovich inequality.

For the bound on the convergence rate we then have

$$1 - \frac{x^t x}{(x^t H x)(x^t H^{-1} x)} \leq 1 - \frac{4\alpha}{(1+\alpha)^2} = \frac{1 - 2\alpha + \alpha^2}{(1+\alpha)^2} = \frac{(1-\alpha)^2}{(1+\alpha)^2}. \qquad \square$$

8.20. By definition of f(x) and F(x) we have

$$F(x) = \nabla f(x)^t \nabla f(x) = (c + Hx)^t (c + Hx) = d^t x + \frac{1}{2} x^t D x,$$

where $d = Hc$ and $D = H^t H = H^2$.

If the steepest descent method is used to find the minimum of F(x), then its rate of convergence is governed by the condition number of the matrix D. More precisely, the rate of convergence is bounded above by $(\beta-1)^2/(\beta+1)^2$, where β is the ratio of the largest to the smallest eigenvalue of D. Since $D = H^2$, eigenvalues od D are squares of eigenvalues of H, hence $\beta = \alpha^2$, where α is the ratio of the largest to the smallest eigenvalue of matrix H. Next, simple algebra yields $(\alpha^2-1)^2/(\alpha^2+1)^2 < (\alpha-1)^2/(\alpha+1)^2$ whenever $\alpha>1$, which implies that the steepest descent method applied to minimization of F(x) will converge at a slower rate than in case of minimization of f(x).

8.33. For notational simplicity subscript j is dropped. That is, we let $D = D_j$, $\nabla f(y) = \nabla f(y_j)$, $q_j = q$, $p = p_j$, $\lambda = \lambda_j$, $\tau = \tau_j$ and $v = v_j$. To avoid misunderstanding, let $\nabla f(y_+) = \nabla f(y_{j+1})$. Furthermore, let $a = \nabla f(y)^t D\nabla f(y)$, $b = \nabla f(y_+)^t D\nabla f(y_+)$, and $c = q^t Dq$. We need to show that there exists a value for ϕ such that $D_+\nabla f(y_+) = 0$. By equations (8.45) and (8.46) we have

$$D_+\nabla f(y_+) = [\, D + \frac{pp^t}{p^tq} - \frac{Dqq^tD}{c} + \phi\tau\frac{vv^t}{p^tq}]\,(q + \nabla f(y)) =$$

$$= Dq + \frac{pp^tq}{p^tq} - \frac{Dqq^tDq}{c} + \phi\tau\frac{vv^tq}{p^tq} + D\nabla f(y) + \frac{pp^t\nabla f(y)}{p^tq} - \frac{Dqq^tD\nabla f(y)}{c} + \phi\tau\frac{vv^t\nabla f(y)}{p^tq} =$$

4

$$= p + D\nabla f(y) + \frac{pp^t\nabla f(y)}{p^tq} - \frac{Dqq^tD\nabla f(y)}{c} + \phi\tau\frac{vv^t\nabla f(y)}{p^tq} \,,$$

where the last step follows from $c=q^t Dq$, $v^tq = 0$. Furthermore, since $p^tq = -p^t\nabla f(y)$, we obtain

$$D_+\nabla f(y_+) = D\nabla f(y) - \frac{Dqq^tD\nabla f(y)}{c} + \phi\tau\frac{vv^t\nabla f(y)}{p^tq} \,.$$

By equations (8.46) and (8.47) we next have

$$\tau\frac{vv^t\nabla f(y)}{p^tq} = \frac{cpp^t\nabla f(y)}{(p^tq)^2} - \frac{pq^tD\nabla f(y)}{p^tq} - \frac{Dqp^t\nabla f(y)}{p^tq} + \frac{Dqq^tD\nabla f(y)}{c}.$$

Now let us note the following relationships:

$$pp^t\nabla f(y) = \lambda^2 aD\nabla f(y), \qquad p^tq = \lambda a, \qquad q^tD\nabla f(y) = -a,$$

$$pq^t D\nabla f(y) = p(\nabla f(y_+) - \nabla f(y))^t D\nabla f(y) = -ap, \text{ and}$$

$$Dqp^t \nabla f(y) = -\lambda D(\nabla f(y_+) - \nabla f(y))\nabla f(y)^t D\nabla f(y) = -\lambda a Dq.$$

Based on the above equations we obtain

$$\tau\frac{vv^t\nabla f(y)}{p^t q} = \tfrac{c}{a}D\nabla f(y) - D\nabla f(y) + Dq - \tfrac{a}{c}Dq.$$

Note that $c = a + b$, which results in $\tau\dfrac{vv^t\nabla f(y)}{p^t q} = \tfrac{b}{a}D\nabla f(y) + \tfrac{b}{c}Dq.$

Therefore,

$$D_+\nabla f(y_+) = D\nabla f(y) + \tfrac{a}{c}Dq + \phi[\tfrac{b}{c}D\nabla f(y) + \tfrac{b}{c}Dq] =$$

$$= (1 + \phi\tfrac{b}{a})D\nabla f(y) + \tfrac{a}{c}(1 + \phi\tfrac{b}{a})Dq = (1 + \phi\tfrac{b}{a})D(\nabla f(y) + \tfrac{a}{c}q).$$

This demonstrates that if $\phi = -\dfrac{a}{b} = -\dfrac{\nabla f(y)^t D\nabla f(y)}{\nabla f(y_+)^t D\nabla f(y_+)}$, then $D_+\nabla f(y_+)$ is automatically

zero, thus completing the proof. $\qquad\qquad\qquad\qquad\qquad\qquad\qquad\qquad\square$

8.55. For notational simplicity let $D = D_j$, and $d = D\nabla f(y_j)$. Then $y_j = y_j - \lambda_j d$, where λ_j

minimizes $f(y_j - \lambda d)$ along direction d. Note that

$$f(y_j - \lambda d) = c^t(y_j - \lambda d) + \tfrac{1}{2}(y_j - \lambda d)^t H(y_j - \lambda d)$$

$$= \tfrac{1}{2}\lambda^2 d^t Hd - \lambda(c+Hy_j)^t d + c^t y_j + \tfrac{1}{2}y_j^t Hy_j$$

5

$$= \tfrac{1}{2}\lambda^2 d^t Hd - \lambda d^t D^{-1}d + c^t y_j + \tfrac{1}{2}y_j^t Hy_j,$$

therefore,

$$\lambda_j = \frac{d^t D^{-1}d}{d^t Hd}. \tag{1}$$

Next let us examine $e(y_{j+1})$:

$$2e(y_{j+1}) = (y_{j+1} - y^*)^t H(y_{j+1} - y^*) = (y_{j+1} - y_j)^t H(y_{j+1} - y_j) + 2(y_{j+1} - y_j)^t H(y_j - y^*)$$

$$+ (y_j - y^*)^t H(y_j - y^*) = \lambda_j^2 d^t Hd - 2\lambda_j d^t D^{-1}d + 2e(y_j).$$

Note that $2e(y_j) = (y_j - y^*)^t H(y_j - y^*) = d^t D^{-1}H^{-1}D^{-1}d$ because $Hy^* + c = 0$, and

$H(y_j - y^*) = -c - Hy_j = -\nabla f(y_j) = -D^{-1}d$. This results together with equation (1) yields

$$e(y_{j+1}) = e(y_j)\left[1 - \frac{(d^t D^{-1}d)^2}{(d^t Hd)(d^t D^{-1}H^{-1}D^{-1}d)}\right]. \tag{2}$$

By assumption, matrix D is symmetric and positive definite. Therefore, there exist an orthogonal matrix Q and a diagonal, positive definite matrix P such that $D = QPPQ^t$. In order to express equation (2) in a more useful way, let $r = P^{-1}Q^t d$ and let $G = PQ^t HQP$. Then

$$d^t D^{-1}d = d^t QP^{-1}P^{-1}Q^t d = r^t r,$$

$$d^t Hd = = d^t QP^{-1}PQ^t HQPP^{-1}Q^t d = r^t PQ^t HQPr = r^t Gr,$$

and $\qquad d^t D^{-1}H^{-1}D^{-1}d = r^t P^{-1}Q^t H^{-1}QP^{-1}r = r^t G^{-1}r,$

which allows us to rewrite equation (2) as

$$e(y_{j+1}) = e(y_j)\left[1 - \frac{(r^t r)^2}{(r^t Gr)(r^t G^{-1}r)}\right].$$

Matrix G is positive definite, hence Kantorovich inequality can be applied to obtain an upper bound on the convergence rate

$$e(y_{j+1}) \le \frac{(\beta - 1)^2}{(\beta + 1)^2}\, e(y_j),$$

where β is the ratio of the largest to the smallest eigenvalue of matrix G. It remains to show that matrices G and DH have the same eigenvalues. For this purpose note that if λ is an eigenvalue of DH and x is a corresponding eigenvector, then $DHx = \lambda x$, and $QPPQ^t Hx = \lambda x$, and furthermore, $PQ^t HQPz = \lambda z$, where $z = P^{-1}Q^t x$. This demonstrates that $Gz = \lambda z$, that is that λ is an eigenvalue of G Therefore, $\beta = \alpha_j$, which completes the proof. $\qquad\square$

ANSWERS TO SELECTED EXERCISES

IN CHAPTER 9

9.3. a. Remark: In the objective function the constant term (110) has been dropped.

$$\text{minimize} \quad f(x) = 4x_1^2 + 4x_2^2 + 10x_1 + 6x_2$$

$$\text{subject to} \quad x_1 + x_2 = 2$$

$$x_1 \geq 0, \ x_2 \geq 0.$$

b. Hessian of the objective function is equal to 8I, thus is positive definite. Therefore, $f(x)$ is strictly convex.

c. The KKT system for the problem in part (a) is:

$$8x_1 \quad - u_1 \quad + v \quad = 10$$

$$8x_2 \quad -u_2 + v = 6$$

$$x_1 + x_2 = 2$$

$$x_1 u_1 = 0, \ x_2 u_2 = 0, \ x_1 \geq 0, \ x_2 \geq 0, \ u_1 \geq 0, \ u_2 \geq 0.$$

The foregoing system has a unique solution: $x_1 = 3/4$, $x_2 = 5/4$, $u_1 = u_2 = 0$, $v = -4$.

d. Penalty function method:

minimize $\{4x_1^2 + 4x_2^2 + 10x_1 + 6x_2 + \mu(x_1 + x_2 - 2)^2 + \mu[\max(-x_1, 0)]^2 + \mu \max[(-x_2, 0)]^2\}$.

Solution (by the steepest descent method):

Let $x = \begin{bmatrix} 0 \\ .5 \end{bmatrix}$ be the starting point.

For each μ, $\nabla f(x) = \begin{bmatrix} 10-3\mu \\ 10-3\mu \end{bmatrix}$, hence $d = \begin{bmatrix} 1 \\ 1 \end{bmatrix}$. Line search step gives $\lambda = \dfrac{-10+3\mu}{8+4\mu}$, therefore,

$x_\mu = \dfrac{1}{8+4\mu} \begin{bmatrix} 3\mu-10 \\ 5\mu-6 \end{bmatrix}$. As $\mu \to \infty$ the sequence $\{x_\mu\}$ converges to $\begin{bmatrix} .75 \\ 1.25 \end{bmatrix}$.

9.5. a. $x^* = (.5, .5)$.

b. Consider $(x_1, x_2) = (-\alpha\mu, 0)$, where $\alpha > 0$. Then the objective function is equal to $-\alpha^3\mu^3 - \alpha\mu^2 - \mu$, and it decreases without bound as $\alpha \to \infty$. Hence, for each $\mu > 0$, the penalty problem is unbounded.

c. Evident.

d. $x_{1\mu} = x_{2\mu} = \dfrac{4}{\sqrt{16 + 24/\mu} + 4} \to \dfrac{1}{2}$ as $\mu \to \infty$.

9.11. For each $\mu > 0$, vector x_μ is an optimal solution for the following penalty problem denoted by (PP):

$$\text{minimize } f(x) + \mu\alpha(x)$$

$$\text{subject to } \quad g_i(x) \leq 0 \text{ for } i = m+1, ..., m+M,$$

$$h_i(x) = 0 \text{ for } i = l+1, ..., l+L,$$

where $\alpha(x) = \displaystyle\sum_{i=1}^{m} \phi[g_i(x)] + \sum_{i=1}^{l} \psi[h_i(x)]$.

Assume that

1. All functions f, g_i, h_i, ϕ and ψ are continuously differentiable.

2. Functions $\phi(.)$ and $\psi(.)$ satisfy (9.1.b), and $\phi'(y) \geq 0$ with $\phi'(y) = 0$ if $y \leq 0$.

3. Assumptions of Theorem 9.2.2 hold, where

$X = \{ x: g_i(x) \leq 0 \text{ for } i = m+1, ..., m+M; \; h_i(x) = 0 \text{ for } i = l+1, ..., l+L \}$.

For each $\mu \geq 0$, vector x_μ solves the penalty problem (PP). Hence, by KKT necessary conditions we can claim the existence of scalars $y_{\mu i}$, $i = m+1, ..., m+M$, and $w_{\mu i}$, $i = l+1, ..., l+L$, that solve the following system:

$$\nabla[f(x_\mu) + \mu\alpha(x_\mu)] + \sum_{i=m+1}^{m+M} y_{\mu i} \, \nabla g_i(x_\mu) + \sum_{i=l+1}^{l+L} w_{\mu i} \, \nabla h_i(x_\mu) = 0,$$

$$y_{\mu i} \, g_i(x_\mu) = 0 \text{ for } \quad i = m+1, ..., m+M,$$

$$y_{\mu i} \geq 0 \text{ for } \qquad i = m+1, ..., m+M.$$

Next, by definition of $\alpha(x)$, we have

$$\nabla[f(x_\mu) + \mu\alpha(x_\mu)] = \nabla f(x_\mu) + \mu\sum_{i=1}^{m} \phi'[g_i(x_\mu)] \, \nabla g_i(x_\mu) + \mu\sum_{i=1}^{l} \psi'[h_i(x_\mu)] \, \nabla h_i(x_\mu).$$

Without loss of generality let $\{x_\mu\} \to \bar{x}$, and let the sets I_0 and I_1 be defined as follows

$$I_0 = \{i: g_i(\bar{x}) = 0\} \cap \{1, ..., m\},$$

$$I_1 = \{i: g_i(\bar{x}) = 0\} \cap \{m+1, ..., m+M\}.$$

For μ large enough we have $g_i(x_\mu) < 0$ for any i that is not in $I_0 \cup I_1$, so that

$$\phi'[g_i(x_\mu)] = 0 \quad \text{if } i \in \{1, ..., m\} \text{ and } i \notin I_0,$$

$$y_{\mu i} = 0 \qquad \text{if } i \in \{m+1, ..., m+M\} \text{ and } i \notin I_1.$$

Therefore, for μ large enough

$$\nabla f(x_\mu) + \mu\sum_{i\in I_0} \phi'[g_i(x_\mu)] \, \nabla g_i(x_\mu) + \mu\sum_{i=1}^{l} \psi'[h_i(x_\mu)] \, \nabla h_i(x_\mu) + \sum_{i\in I_1} y_{\mu i} \, \nabla g_i(x_\mu)$$

$$+ \sum_{i=l+1}^{l+L} w_{\mu i} \, \nabla h_i(x_\mu) = 0.$$

Let

$$u_{\mu i} = \begin{cases} \mu \, \phi'[g_i(x_\mu)] & \text{if } i \in I_0 \\ y_{\mu i} & \text{if } i \in I_1 \\ 0 & \text{if } i \notin I_0 \cup I_1 \end{cases}$$

$$v_{\mu i} = \begin{cases} \mu \, \psi'[h_i(x_\mu)] & \text{for } i = 1, ..., l \\ \\ w_{\mu i} & \text{for } i = l+1, ..., l+L. \end{cases}$$

Notice that $u_{\mu i} \geq 0$ for $i = 1, ..., m+M$.

Since $\{x_\mu\} \to \bar{x}$ and all functions in the last equation are continuous, values of Lagrange multipliers $\bar{u}_i$, $\bar{v}_i$ at $\bar{x}$ can then be retrieved by employing limits:

$$\bar{u}_i = \lim_{\mu \to \infty} u_{\mu i} \quad \text{for } i = 1, ..., m+M,$$

$$\bar{v}_i = \lim_{\mu \to \infty} v_{\mu i} \quad \text{for } i = 1, ..., l+L.$$

9.12. First let us note that by the definition of $F_E(x)$, all that we need to show is that $\bar{x}$ is a local minimizer for the following problem, denoted by (EPP):

minimize $\quad f(x) + \mu(\sum_{i=1}^{m} y_i + \sum_{i=1}^{l} z_i)$

subject to $\qquad y_i \geq g_i(x) \quad$ for $i = 1, ..., m$

$\qquad\qquad z_i \geq h_i(x) \quad$ and $\quad z_i \geq -h_i(x) \quad$ for $i = 1, ..., l$

$\qquad\qquad y_i \geq 0 \quad$ for $i = 1, ..., m$.

We show that under the assumptions listed in this problem, vector $\bar{x}$ meets sufficient conditions for a local minimizer in problem (EPP) as given by Theorem 4.2.2.

For this purpose we first show that if

$\quad \bar{y}_i = \max \{0, g_i(\bar{x})\} \quad$ for $\quad i = 1, ..., m \qquad\qquad$ (a)

$\quad \bar{z}_i = \max \{ h_i(\bar{x}), -h_i(\bar{x})\} \quad$ for $\quad i = 1, ..., l \qquad$ (b)

then $(\bar{x}, \bar{y}, \bar{z})$ is a KKT point for the problem (EPP).

A vector $(\bar{x}, \bar{y}, \bar{z})$ is a KKT point for (EPP) if there exist scalars u_i^+, u_i^-, v_i^+ and v_i^-, associated with constraints $g_i(x) - y_i \leq 0$, $y_i \geq 0$, $h_i(x) \leq 0$ and $-h_i(x) \leq 0$, respectively, such that

$$\nabla f(\bar{x}) + \sum_{i=1}^{m} u_i^+ \nabla g_i(\bar{x}) + \sum_{i=1}^{l} (v_i^+ - v_i^-) \nabla h_i(\bar{x}) = 0$$

$\mu - u_i^+ - u_i^- = 0$ for $i = 1, ..., m$

$\mu - v_i^+ - v_i^- = 0$ for $i = 1, ..., l$

$u_i^+ \geq 0$ and $u_i^- \geq 0$ for $i = 1, ..., m \qquad\qquad$ (c)

$v_i^+ \geq 0$ and $v_i^- \geq 0$ for $i = 1, ..., l$

$u_i^+ = 0$ for $i \notin I_\mu$,

where I_μ is the set of indices of constraints that are binding at $(\bar{x}, \bar{y}, \bar{z})$.

Notice that since $\bar{x}$ is a feasible solution for the original problem, we necessarily have $g_i(\bar{x}) \leq 0$ for $i = 1, ..., m$, and $h_i(\bar{x}) = 0$ for $i = 1, ..., l$, which by equations (a) and (b) implies that $\bar{y}_i = 0$ for $i = 1, ..., m$ as well as $\bar{z}_i = 0$ for $i = 1, ..., l$. This further leads to the conclusion that the only constraints of the problem (EPP) that are not active at $(\overline{x}, \overline{y}, \overline{z})$ are inequalities $y_i \geq g_i(x)$ for $i \notin I = \{i: g_i(\overline{x}) = 0\}$. Let $\mu \geq$ maximum $\{\ \overline{u}_i, i \in I,\ |\overline{v}_i|, i = 1, ..., l\}$, where $\overline{u}_i$, $i = 1, ...,$ m, and $\overline{v}_i$, $i = 1, ..., l$ are Lagrange multipliers for the problem P associated with $\overline{x}$. Next, let

$$\overline{u}_i^+ = \overline{u}_i \quad \text{if } i \in I \quad \text{and} \quad \overline{u}_i^+ = 0 \quad \text{if } i \notin I$$

$$\overline{u}_i^- = \mu - \overline{u}_i^+ \text{ for } \quad i = 1, ..., m$$

$$\overline{v}_i^+ = \tfrac{1}{2}(\mu + \overline{v}_i) \text{ for } \quad i = 1, ..., l$$

$$\overline{v}_i^- = \tfrac{1}{2}(\mu - \overline{v}_i) \text{ for } \quad i = 1, ..., l.$$

It can be easily verified that the above $\overline{u}^+, \overline{u}^-, \overline{v}^+$ and $\overline{v}^-$ solve the KKT system (c). Therefore, $(\overline{x}, \overline{y}, \overline{z})$ is a KKT point for the problem (EPP).

Next we need to show that the Hessian matrix of the restricted Lagrange function for the problem (EPP) is positive definite on the cone C_μ. For notational simplicity and without loss of generality let us consider $\mu >$ maximum $\{\ \overline{u}_i, i \in I,\ |\overline{v}_i|, i = 1, ..., l\}$. In this case Lagrange multipliers $\overline{u}^-$, $\overline{v}^+$ and $\overline{v}^-$ all take positive values. Next, let us define the following sets

$$I^+ = \{i: i \in I, \overline{u}_i > 0\} \text{ and } I^0 = \{i: i \in I, \overline{u}_i = 0\},$$

and notice that $\overline{u}_i^+ > 0$ only if $i \in I^+$.

The cone C_μ is the cone of all nonzero vectors $[d_x^t\ d_y^t\ d_z^t]$ such that

$$\nabla g_i(x)^t d_x - e_i^t d_y = 0 \qquad\qquad \text{for } i \in I^+,$$

$$-e_i^t d_y = 0 \qquad\qquad \text{for } i = 1, ..., m,$$

$$\nabla h_i(x)^t d_x - e_i^t d_z = 0 \qquad\qquad \text{for } i = 1, ..., l,$$

$$-\nabla h_i(x)^t d_x - e_i^t d_z = 0 \qquad\qquad \text{for } i = 1, ..., l,$$

$$\nabla g_i(x)^t d_x - e_i^t d_y \leq 0 \qquad\qquad \text{for } i \in I^0.$$

Since $-e_i^t d_y = 0$ for $i = 1, ..., m$, we necessarily obtain $d_y = 0$, and furthermore, the last and the first of the above conditions reduce to $\nabla g_i(x)^t d_x = 0$ for $i \in I^+$ and $\nabla g_i(x)^t d_x \leq 0$ for $i \in I^0$, respectively. Moreover, the third and fourth conditions yield $d_z = 0$, and $\nabla h_i(x)^t d_x = 0$ for $i = 1, ..., l$. This allows us to conclude that the cone C_μ is the cone of all nonzero vectors $[d^t\ 0^t\ 0^t]$ such that

$\nabla g_i(x)^t d = 0$ for $i \in I^+$, $\nabla g_i(x)^t d \leq 0$ for $i \in I^0$, and $\nabla h_i(x)^t d = 0$ for $i = 1, ..., l$. (d)

Next let us turn to the Hessian matrix of the restricted Lagrange function $L(x, y, z)$ for the problem (EPP), where by (4.25)

$$L(x, y, z) = f(x) + \mu(\sum_{i=1}^{m} y_i + \sum_{i=1}^{l} z_i) + \sum_{i \in I} \overline{u}_i^+ (g_i(x) - y_i) - \sum_{i=1}^{m} \overline{u}_i^- y_i$$

$$+ \sum_{i=1}^{l} \overline{v}_i^+ (h_i(x) - z_i) - \sum_{i=1}^{l} \overline{v}_i^- (h_i(x) + z_i).$$

Therefore, the Hessian matrix $\nabla^2 L(\overline{x}, \overline{y}, \overline{z})$ of $L(x, y, z)$ evaluated at $(\overline{x}, \overline{y}, \overline{z})$ is

$$\nabla^2 L(\overline{x}, \overline{y}, \overline{z}) = \begin{bmatrix} L_1 & 0 & 0 \\ 0 & 0 & 0 \\ 0 & 0 & 0 \end{bmatrix},$$

where $L_1 = \nabla^2 f(\overline{x}) + \sum_{i \in I} \overline{u}_i^+ \nabla^2 g_i(\overline{x}) + \sum_{i=1}^{l} (\overline{v}_i^+ - \overline{v}_i^-) \nabla^2 h_i(\overline{x})$, and the remaining blocks are zero matrices of appropriate sizes.

Now let us examine the quadratic form $[d_x^t \ d_y^t \ d_z^t]\nabla^2 L(\overline{x}, \overline{y}, \overline{z}) [d_x^t \ d_y^t \ d_z^t]^t$. Due to the structure of $\nabla^2 L(\overline{x}, \overline{y}, \overline{z})$ we obtain

$$[d_x^t \ d_y^t \ d_z^t]\nabla^2 L(\overline{x}, \overline{y}, \overline{z}) [d_x^t \ d_y^t \ d_z^t]^t = d_x^t L_1 d_x$$

$$= d_x^t [\nabla^2 f(\overline{x}) + \sum_{i \in I} \overline{u}_i^+ \nabla^2 g_i(\overline{x}) + \sum_{i=1}^{l} (\overline{v}_i^+ - \overline{v}_i^-) \nabla^2 h_i(\overline{x})] d_x$$

$$= d_x^t [\nabla^2 f(\overline{x}) + \sum_{i \in I} \overline{u}_i \nabla^2 g_i(\overline{x}) + \sum_{i=1}^{l} \overline{v}_i \nabla^2 h_i(\overline{x})] d_x = d^t \nabla^2 L(\overline{x}) d,$$

where $L(x)$ is the restricted Lagrange function for the problem P, and $d = d_x$.

The last quadratic form is known to be positive for all nonzero vectors d such that $\nabla g_i(x)^t d = 0$ for $i \in I^+$, $\nabla g_i(x)^t d \leq 0$ for $i \in I^0$, and $\nabla h_i(x)^t d = 0$ for $i = 1, ..., l$, since $\overline{x}$ meets second order sufficient conditions as given in Theorem 4.2.2. By equation (d), we can thus assert that the Hessian of the restricted Lagrange function $L(x, y, z)$ at $(\overline{x}, \overline{y}, \overline{z})$ for the problem (EPP) is positive definite on the cone C_μ. Therefore, $(\overline{x}, \overline{y}, \overline{z})$ satisfies all assumptions of Theorem 4.2.2

for the problem (EPP), and hence it is its local minimizer . This means that $\overline{x}$ is a local minimizer of the function F_E, which completes the proof. $\square$

9.16. $\overline{x}$ is a KKT point for P, and $\overline{u}$ and $\overline{v}$ are the corresponding Lagrange multipliers. Therefore,

$$\nabla f(\overline{x}) + \sum_{i=1}^{m} \overline{u}_i \nabla g_i(\overline{x}) + \sum_{i=1}^{l} \overline{v}_i \nabla h_i(\overline{x}) = 0$$

$g_i(\overline{x}) \le 0$ for $i = 1, ..., m$

$h_i(\overline{x}) = 0$ for $i = 1, ..., l$

$\overline{u}_i g_i(\overline{x}) = 0$ and $u_i \ge 0$ for $i = 1, ..., m$.

Since the second order sufficiency conditions are met at $(\overline{x}, \overline{u}, \overline{v})$ and strict complementarity condition holds (so that $I^+ = I$ in Theorem 4.4.2), we have

$d^t \nabla^2 L(\overline{x}) d > 0$ for all $d \in C = \{d \ne 0, \nabla g_i(\overline{x})^t d = 0$ for $i \in I, \nabla h_i(\overline{x})^t d = 0$ for $i = 1, ..., l\}$.

The KKT conditions for problem P' are:

$$\nabla f(x) + \sum_{i=1}^{m} u_i \nabla g_i(x) + \sum_{i=1}^{l} v_i \nabla h_i(x) = 0$$

$2s_i u_i = 0$ for $i = 1, ..., m$

$g_i(x) + s_i^2 = 0$ for $i = 1, ..., m$

$h_i(x) = 0$ for $i = 1, ..., l$

Readily, if $\overline{x}, \overline{u}, \overline{v}$ is a KKT point for P, then $\overline{x}, \overline{s}, \overline{u}, \overline{v}$, where $\overline{s}_i^2 = g_i(\overline{x})$, $i = 1, ..., m$, is a KKT point for P'. The Hessian of the restricted Lagrangian function is $H(\overline{x}, \overline{s}) = \begin{bmatrix} \nabla^2 L(\overline{x}) & 0 \\ 0 & D \end{bmatrix}$, where D is a diagonal matrix with $2\overline{u}_i$, $i = 1, ..., m$, on the diagonal. We need to show that the quadratic form $[d_x^t \ d_s^t] H \begin{bmatrix} d_x \\ d_s \end{bmatrix}$ is positive definite on the cone

$$C' = \left\{ \begin{bmatrix} d_x \\ d_s \end{bmatrix} \ne \begin{bmatrix} 0 \\ 0 \end{bmatrix} : \nabla g_i(\overline{x})^t d_x + 2\overline{s}_i d_{i_s} = 0 \text{ for } i = 1, ..., m, \nabla h_i(\overline{x})^t d_x = 0 \text{ for } i = 1, ..., l \right\}.$$

Note that by the strict complementarity condition and definition of s, we have $\overline{s}_i = 0$ and $\overline{u}_i > 0$ for each $i \in I$. Also, $\overline{u}_i = 0$ and $\overline{s}_i \ne 0$ for $i \notin I$. Therefore,

$$[d_x^t \ d_s^t] H \begin{bmatrix} d_x \\ d_s \end{bmatrix} = d_x^t \nabla^2 L(\overline{x}) d_x + 2\sum_{i=1}^{m} d_{i_s}^2 \overline{u}_i = d_x^t \nabla^2 L(\overline{x}) d_x + 2\sum_{i \in I} d_{i_s}^2 \overline{u}_i,$$

and the system

$$\nabla g_i(\overline{x})^t d_x + 2\overline{s}_i d_{i_s} = 0 \text{ for } i = 1, ..., m,$$

is equivalent to

$$\nabla g_i(\overline{x})^t d_x = 0 \text{ for } i \in I,$$

$$\nabla g_i(\overline{x})^t d_x + 2\overline{s}_i d_{i_s} = 0 \text{ for } i \notin I.$$

Finally note that $d_x^t \nabla^2 L(\overline{x}) d_x + 2\sum_{i \in I} d_{i_s}^2 \overline{u}_i > 0$ for any $\begin{bmatrix} d_x \\ d_s \end{bmatrix}$ such that $d_x \in C$, and that if vector $\begin{bmatrix} d_x \\ d_s \end{bmatrix} \in C'$ then $d_x \in C$. Therefore, $H(\overline{x}, \overline{s})$ is positive definite on the cone C', which completes the proof. $\qquad\qquad\qquad\qquad\square$

If the strict complementarity condition does not hold, then $H(\overline{x}, \overline{s})$ is positive semidefinite on the cone C'.

9.17. Let

$$F_{ALAG}(x,u,v) = f(x) + \mu \sum_{i=1}^m \max^2\{g_i(x) + \frac{u_i}{2\mu}, 0\} - \sum_{i=1}^m \frac{u_i^2}{4\mu} + \sum_{i=1}^l v_i h_i(x) + \mu \sum_{i=1}^l h_i^2(x).$$

By assumption, x_k minimizes $F_{ALAG}(x,\overline{u},\overline{v})$, where $\overline{u}$ and $\overline{v}$ are given vectors, so that $\nabla_x F_{ALAG}(x_k,\overline{u},\overline{v}) = 0$. This means that

$$\nabla f(x_k) + 2\mu \sum_{i=1}^m (g_i(x_k) + \frac{\overline{u}_i}{2\mu}) \nabla g_i(x_k) + \sum_{i=1}^l \overline{v}_i \nabla h_i(x_k) + 2\mu \sum_{i=1}^l h_i(x_k)\nabla h(x_k) = 0,$$

or equivalently,

$$\nabla f(x_k) + 2\mu \sum_{i=1}^m (g_i(x_k) + \frac{\overline{u}_i}{2\mu}) \nabla g_i(x_k) + \sum_{i=1}^l (\overline{v}_i + 2\mu h_i(x_k))\nabla h_i(x_k) = 0. \qquad (a)$$

If $L(x, u, v) = f(x) + \sum_{i=1}^m u_i g_i(x) + \sum_{i=1}^l v_i h_i(x)$, then

$$\nabla_x L(x_k, \overline{u}_{new}, \overline{v}_{new}) = \nabla f(x_k) + \sum_{i=1}^m (\overline{u}_{new})_i \nabla g_i(x_k) + \sum_{i=1}^l (\overline{v}_{new})_i \nabla h_i(x_k).$$

The requirement that $\nabla_x L(x_k, \overline{u}_{new}, \overline{v}_{new}) = 0$ together with equation (a) (known to hold) yields the following expressions for $\overline{u}_{new}$ and $\overline{v}_{new}$:

$$(\overline{u}_{new})_i = \begin{cases} 2\mu g_i(x_k) + \overline{u}_i & \text{if } 2\mu g_i(x_k) + \overline{u}_i > 0 \\ \\ 0 & \text{otherwise} \end{cases}$$

$$(\overline{v}_{new})_i = \overline{v}_i + 2\mu h_i(x_k).$$

Simple algebra leads to

$$(\overline{u}_{new})_i = \overline{u}_i + \max\{2\mu g_i(x_k), -\overline{u}_i\} \quad \text{for} \quad i = 1, ..., m.$$

This shows that $\overline{u}_{new}$ and $\overline{v}_{new}$ are as given by equations (9.27) and (9.19) respectively. □

9.18. The corresponding barrier problem is:

minimize $\quad f(x) + \mu\sum_{i=1}^{m} \phi[g_i(x)]$

subject to $\quad g_i(x) < 0 \;$ for $\; i = 1, ..., m,$

$\qquad\qquad g_i(x) \leq 0 \;$ for $\; i = m+1, ..., m+M,$

$\qquad\qquad h_i(x) = 0 \;$ for $\; i = 1, ..., l.$

Assume the following:

1. Function ϕ satisfies (9.28) and is continuously differentiable.

2. Functions f, g_i, i = 1, ..., m+M, and $h_i(x)$, i = 1, ..., l are continuously differentiable.

3. Assumptions of Lemma 9.4.2 and Theorem 9.4.3 hold with

$$X = \{\; x: g_i(x) \leq 0,\, i = m+1, ..., m+M,\, h_i(x) = 0,\, i = 1, ..., l\}.$$

4. Optimal solution $\overline{x}$ to the problem

$\quad$ min $\{f(x) : g_i(x) \leq 0,\, i = 1, ..., \; m+M,\, h_i(x) = 0,\, i = 1, ..., l\}$

obtained as an accumulation point of the sequence $\{x_\mu\}$ is a regular point.

For simplicity, and without loss of generality, consider the case when $\{x_\mu\}$ itself converges to $\overline{x}$.

Define two sets I_0 and I_1 :

$$I_0 = \{\; i: g_i(\overline{x}) = 0\} \cap \{\; 1, ..., m\}$$

$$I_1 = \{\; i: g_i(\overline{x}) = 0\} \cap \{\; m+1, ..., m+M\}.$$

There exist unique Lagrange multipliers $\bar{u}_i$, i = 1, ..., m+M and $\bar{v}_i$, i = 1, ..., l such that

$$\nabla f(\bar{x}) + \sum_{i=1}^{m} \bar{u}_i \, \nabla g_i(\bar{x}) + \sum_{i=m+1}^{m+M} \bar{u}_i \, \nabla g_i(\bar{x}) + \sum_{i=1}^{l} \bar{v}_i \nabla h_i(\bar{x}) = 0$$

$$\bar{u}_i \geq 0 \text{ for } i = 1, ..., m+M$$

$$\bar{u}_i = 0 \text{ for } i \in I_0 \cup I_1.$$

By assumption, x_μ solves the barrier problem, and hence for each $\mu > 0$ there exist unique Lagrange multipliers $y_{\mu i}$, i = m+1, ..., m+M, and $w_{\mu i}$, i = 1, ..., l such that

$$\nabla f(x_\mu) + \mu \sum_{i=1}^{m} \phi'([g_i(x_\mu)]\nabla g_i(x_\mu) + \sum_{i=m+1}^{m+M} y_{\mu i} \, \nabla g_i(x_\mu) + \sum_{i=1}^{l} w_{\mu i} \, \nabla h_i(x_\mu) = 0,$$

$$y_{\mu i} \geq 0 \text{ for } i = m+1, ..., m+M,$$

$$y_{\mu i} g_i(x_\mu) = 0 \text{ for } i = m+1, ..., m+M.$$

By assumption $\{x_\mu\} \to \bar{x}$ as $\mu \to 0^+$, so that we obtain

$$\{\nabla f(x_\mu)\} \to \nabla f(\bar{x}),$$

$$\{\nabla g_i(x_\mu)\} \to \nabla g_i(\bar{x}) \text{ for } i = 1, ..., m+M, \quad \{\nabla h_i(x_\mu)\} \to \nabla h_i(\bar{x}) \text{ for } i = 1, ..., l,$$

$$\{\phi'([g_i(x_\mu)]\} \to y_i \geq 0 \text{ for } i = 1, ..., m, \text{ where } y_i = 0 \text{ if } i \notin I_0$$

$$\{y_{\mu i}\} \to y_i \geq 0 \text{ for } i = m+1, ..., m+M, \text{ where } y_i = 0 \text{ if } i \notin I_1.$$

$$\{w_{\mu i}\} \to w_i \text{ for } i = 1, ..., l.$$

This means that $\bar{x}$, y_i, i = 1, ..., m+M and w_i, i = 1, ..., l satisfy the following system

$$\nabla f(\bar{x}) + \sum_{i=1}^{m} y_i \nabla g_i(\bar{x}) + \sum_{i=m+1}^{m+M} y_i \, \nabla g_i(\bar{x}) + \sum_{i=1}^{l} w_i \nabla h_i(\bar{x}) = 0,$$

$$y_i \geq 0 \text{ for } i = 1, ..., m+M$$

$$y_i = 0 \text{ for } i \notin I_0 \cap I_1.$$

From the foregoing analysis it follows that the unique Lagrange multipliers $\bar{u}_i$, i = 1, ..., m+M and $\bar{v}_i$, i = 1, ..., l can be derived as limits of $\{y_{\mu i}\}$ and $\{w_{\mu i}\}$, respectively. That is,

$$\bar{u}_i = \lim_{\mu \to 0^+} \mu \phi'[g_i(x_\mu)] \text{ for } i = 1, ..., m,$$

$$\bar{u}_i = \lim_{\mu \to 0^+} y_{\mu i} \text{ for } i = m+1, ..., m+M,$$

$$\overline{v}_i = \lim_{\mu \to 0^+} w_{\mu i} \text{ for } i = 1, ..., l.$$

9.30. For the problem in Example 9.51, where $A = [\, 1 \quad 2\,]$, $b = 2$, we obtain the following simplified

closed form expressions for direction vectors d_v, d_u, and d_x at $\overline{v}$, $\overline{u}$ and $\overline{x}$, respectively:

$$d_v = -\frac{2}{\alpha(\overline{x})}(\beta - 1)\overline{\mu}, \qquad d_u = -\begin{bmatrix} 1 \\ 2 \end{bmatrix} d_v,$$

$$d_x = (\beta - 1)\left(\begin{bmatrix} \overline{x}_1 \\ \overline{x}_2 \end{bmatrix} - \frac{2}{\alpha(\overline{x})} \begin{bmatrix} \overline{x}_1^2 \\ 2\overline{x}_2^2 \end{bmatrix} \right),$$

where $\alpha(\overline{x}) = \overline{x}_1^2 + 4\overline{x}_2^2$.

Based on the above expressions, we have

$$\hat{x} = \beta \begin{bmatrix} \overline{x}_1 \\ \overline{x}_2 \end{bmatrix} - \frac{2(\beta-1)}{\alpha(\overline{x})} \begin{bmatrix} \overline{x}_1^2 \\ 2\overline{x}_2^2 \end{bmatrix}, \quad \hat{u} = \begin{bmatrix} \overline{u}_1 \\ \overline{u}_2 \end{bmatrix} + \frac{2\overline{\mu}(\beta-1)}{\alpha(\overline{x})} \begin{bmatrix} 1 \\ 2 \end{bmatrix},$$

$$\hat{v} = \overline{v} - \frac{2\overline{\mu}(\beta-1)}{\alpha(\overline{x})}.$$

Below, for notational simplicity, we write vectors x and u as row vectors (instead of column

vectors).

If the starting vectors are $x_0 = [\, 2/9 \quad 8/9\,]$, $u_0 = [4 \quad 1]$, $\mu_0 = 8/9$, and $v_0 = -1$, then

the first ten iterations of the primal-dual path following algorithm produce the following results:

Iteration 1.

$x_1 = \hat{x} = [\, .174840038 \quad .91257998\,]$, $\quad u_1 = \hat{u} = [\, 3.862930111 \quad .725860221\,]$,

$v_1 = \hat{v} = -.86293011$; $\quad \mu_1 = \hat{\mu} = \beta\overline{\mu} = .6689$.

Iteration 2.

$x_2 = \hat{x} = [\, .0035539361 \quad .931964893\,]$, $\quad u_2 = \hat{u} = [\, 3.764443977 \quad .528887953\,]$,

$v_2 = \hat{v} = -.764443976$; $\quad \mu_2 = \hat{\mu} = \beta\overline{\mu} = .503355745$.

Iteration 3.

$x_3 = \hat{x} = [\ .002676181 \quad .948801817\ ], \quad u_3 = \hat{u} = [\ 3.69273108 \quad .385462159\ ],$

$v_3 = \hat{v} = -.692731079; \quad \mu_3 = \hat{\mu} = \beta\overline{\mu} = .37878159.$

Iteration 4.

$x_4 = \hat{x} = [\ .002014844 \quad .96147223\ ], \quad u_4 = \hat{u} = [\ 3.640664398 \quad .281328794\ ],$

$v_4 = \hat{v} = -.640664396; \quad \mu_4 = \hat{\mu} = \beta\overline{\mu} = .285037957.$

Iteration 5.

$x_5 = \hat{x} = [\ .001516739 \quad .971007092\ ], \quad u_5 = \hat{u} = [\ 3.602509381 \quad .205018759\ ],$

$v_5 = \hat{v} = -.602509379; \quad \mu_5 = \hat{\mu} = \beta\overline{\mu} = .214494682.$

Iteration 6.

$x_6 = \hat{x} = [\ .001141667 \quad .978182317\ ], \quad u_6 = \hat{u} = [\ 3.574358345 \quad .148716687\ ],$

$v_6 = \hat{v} = -.574358343; \quad \mu_6 = \hat{\mu} = \beta\overline{\mu} = .161409972.$

Iteration 7.

$x_7 = \hat{x} = [\ .000859287 \quad .983581832\ ], \quad u_7 = \hat{u} = [\ 3.553483968 \quad .106967933\ ],$

$v_7 = \hat{v} = -.553483966; \quad \mu_7 = \hat{\mu} = \beta\overline{\mu} = .121463053.$

Iteration 8.

$x_8 = \hat{x} = [\ .000646718 \quad .987645071\ ], \quad u_8 = \hat{u} = [\ 3.537947724 \quad .075895444\ ],$

$v_8 = \hat{v} = -.537947722; \quad \mu_8 = \hat{\mu} = \beta\overline{\mu} = .091402489.$

Iteration 9.

$x_9 = \hat{x} = [\ .000486716 \quad .99070273\ ], \quad u_9 = \hat{u} = [\ 3.526352501 \quad .052704998\ ],$

$v_9 = \hat{v} = -.526352499; \quad \mu_9 = \hat{\mu} = \beta\overline{\mu} = .068751533.$

Iteration 10.

$x_{10} = \hat{x} = [\ .000366289 \quad .993003671\ ], \quad u_{10} = \hat{u} = [\ 3.517684508 \quad .035369011\ ],$

$v_{10} = \hat{v} = -.517684505; \quad \hat{\mu} = \beta\overline{\mu} = .068751533.$

If $\epsilon \geq .15$, then since $n\overline{\mu} = 2\hat{\mu} = .137503066$, the last iterate can be accepted as an approximation of the optimal solution to this problem. The optimal solution is $x^* = [0\ \ 1]$.

ANSWERS TO SELECTED EXERCISES

IN CHAPTER 10

10.3. a. If $\hat{x}$ is a Fritz John point for the problem min $\{f(x) : g_i(x) \leq 0, i = 1, ..., m\}$,

then there exists a vector u_I, where $I = \{i: g_i(\hat{x}) = 0\}$, and a scalar u_0 such that

$$\nabla f(\hat{x}) u_0 + \sum_{i \in I} u_i \nabla g_i(\hat{x}) = 0$$

$u_0 \geq 0, \quad u_i \geq 0$

$(u_0, u_i) \neq (0, 0).$

This means that the system $A^t y = 0$, $y \geq 0$, $y \neq 0$, where columns of A^t are $\nabla f(\hat{x})$ and $\nabla g_i(\hat{x})$,

$i \in I$, has a solution (here, $y = [u_0 \ u_1 \ ... \ u_m]^t$). Therefore, by Gordan's Theorem, the system

$Ad < 0$ has no solution. That is, no (nonzero) vector d exists such that $\nabla f(\hat{x})^t d < 0$ and

$\nabla g_i(\hat{x})^t d < 0$, $i \in I$. This implies that the feasible set in the problem:

minimize z

subject to $\quad \nabla f(\hat{x})^t d \leq z$

$\nabla g_i(\hat{x})^t d \leq z$ for $i \in I$,

$d_i \geq -1 \quad$ if $\dfrac{\delta f(\hat{x})}{\delta x_i} > 0$

$d_i \leq 1 \quad$ if $\dfrac{\delta f(\hat{x})}{\delta x_i} < 0$

has no point for which z<0. However, $(\hat{z}, \hat{d}) = (0, 0)$ is a feasible solution for this problem, and

therefore, it must be optimal.

Same arguments can be used to show that if $(\hat{z}, \hat{d}) = (0, 0)$ solves the foregoing problem, then $\hat{x}$

is a Fritz John point for the problem min $\{f(x) : g_i(x) \leq 0, i = 1, ..., m\}$.

b. By the problem formulation, we have $\hat{z} = \max \{\nabla f(\hat{x})^t d \ , \ \nabla g_i(\hat{x})^t d \ , \ i \in I\}$. Since $\hat{z} < 0$, we

necessarily have $\nabla f(\hat{x})^t d < 0$. Therefore, d is an improving direction of f(x) at $\hat{x}$. Furthermore, since $\quad \nabla g_i(\hat{x})^t d < 0$, $i \in I$, there exists $\lambda > 0$ such that $g_i(\hat{x} + \lambda d) \leq 0$ for any $\lambda \in (0, \lambda)$, i = 1, ..., m, so that d is also a feasible direction at $\hat{x}$. This shows that d is an improving feasible direction at $\hat{x}$. $\qquad\square$

c. Select $k \in I$, and use the following bounding constraints:

$$d_i \geq -1 \quad \text{if } \frac{\delta g_k(\hat{x})}{\delta x_i} > 0$$

$$d_i \leq 1 \quad \text{if } \frac{\delta g_k(\hat{x})}{\delta x_i} < 0.$$

10.12. a. Direction-finding problem decomposes into n (independent) linear one-dimensional problems, one for each d_j. In a jth problem, the function $\nabla_j d_j$ is minimized over the interval

$$[-1, 1] \quad \text{if } a_j < x_j < b_j$$

$$[0, 1] \quad \text{if } x_j = a_j$$

$$[-1, 0] \quad \text{if } x_j = b_j.$$

Therefore, the optimal solution is :

$$d_j = 1 \quad \text{if } \nabla_j < 0 \text{ and } x_j < b_j$$

$$d_j = -1 \quad \text{if } \nabla_j > 0 \text{ and } x_j > a_j$$

$$d_j = 0 \quad \text{otherwise.}$$

b. Assume that $\nabla_j \neq 0$ for at least one j. Direction-finding problem is

minimize $\quad \displaystyle\sum_{i=1}^{n} \nabla_j d_j$

subject to

$$d_j \leq 0 \quad \text{for j such that } x_j = b_j$$

$$d_j \geq 0 \quad \text{for j such that } x_j = a_j$$

$$\sum_{i=1}^{n} d_j^2 \leq 1.$$

It can be easily verified that vector $d^* = [d_j^*]$, where

$$d_j^* = \begin{cases} -\nabla_j / \sum_{j \in J} \nabla_j^2 & \text{if } j \in J \\ \\ 0 & \text{if } j \notin J, \end{cases}$$

and where $J = \{j : x_j > a_j \text{ and } \nabla_j \geq 0, \text{ or else } x_j < b_j \text{ and } \nabla_j < 0\}$ is a feasible solution to this

problem. In order to prove that d^* is an optimal solution we first show that vector d^* is a KKT

point for this problem. For this purpose, let u_j, for j such that $x_j = b_j$ or $x_j = a_j$, and w denote

Lagrange multipliers associated with the constraints $d_j \leq 0$, $d_j \geq 0$ and

$\sum_{i=1}^{n} d_j^2 \leq 1$, respectively. The KKT system is:

$$\nabla_j + u_j + 2wd_j = 0 \text{ for j such that } x_j = b_j$$

$$\nabla_j - u_j + 2wd_j = 0 \text{ for j such that } x_j = a_j$$

$$\nabla_j + 2wd_j = 0 \text{ for all remaining } js$$

$$u_j d_j = 0 \text{ and } u_j \geq 0 \text{ for all js such that } x_j = a_j \text{ or } x_j = b_j$$

$$w\left(\sum_{i=1}^{n} d_j^2 - 1 \right) = 0 , \quad w \geq 0.$$

It can be easily verified that if $d_j = d_j^*$, $j = 1, ..., n$, then

$$u_j = 0 \text{ if } j \in J$$

$$u_j = -\nabla_j \text{ if } j \notin J \text{ and } \nabla_j < 0$$

$$u_j = \nabla_j \text{ if } j \notin J \text{ and } \nabla_j \geq 0$$

$$w = \left(\sum_{j \in J} \nabla_j^2 \right)^{1/2}$$

solve the KKT system for this problem. Therefore, d^* is a KKT point for the direction-finding

problem. Furthermore, the objective function in this problem is linear (hence pseudoconvex), and

all the constraint functions are quasiconvex. Therefore, by Theorem 4.3.8 we can assert that d^* is

an optimal solution. ◻

c. For notational convenience all vectors are given as row vectors.

Method in part (a) produces the following results:

Iteration 1.

$x_1 = [-3 \quad -4]$, $\nabla f(x_1) = [-11 \quad -23]$, $f(x_1) = 71$

$d_1 = [1 \quad 1]$, $\lambda_1 = \min\{17/4, 3\} = 3$.

Iteration 2.

$x_2 = [0 \quad -1]$, $\nabla f(x_2) = [-2 \quad -8]$, $f(x_2) = 5$

$d_2 = [0 \quad 1]$, $\lambda_2 = \min\{4/3, 2\} = 4/3$.

Iteration 3.

$x_3 = [0 \quad 1/3]$, $\nabla f(x_3) = [-10/3 \quad 0]$, $f(x_3) = -1/3$

$d_3 = [0 \quad -1]$. The inner product of $\nabla f(x_3)$ and d_3 is zero. STOP. Vector $[0 \quad 1/3]$ is a KKT point for this problem. Since assumptions of Theorem 4.3.8 hold we can conclude that it is an optimal solution.

Method in part (b) produces the same sequence of iterates:

Iteration 1.

$x_1 = [-3 \quad -4]$, $\nabla f(x_1) = [-11 \quad -23]$, $f(x_1) = 71$, $I = \{1, 2\}$

$d_1 = \frac{1}{\sqrt{650}} [11 \quad 23]$, $\lambda_1 = \min\{\frac{650}{315}\sqrt{650}, 3\} = 3$.

Iteration 2.

$x_2 = [0 \quad -1]$, $\nabla f(x_2) = [-2 \quad -8]$, $f(x_2) = 5$, $I = \{2\}$

$d_2 = [0 \quad 1]$, $\lambda_2 = \min\{4/3, 2\} = 4/3$.

Iteration 3.

$x_3 = [0 \quad 1/3]$, $\nabla f(x_3) = [-10/3 \quad 0]$, $f(x_3) = -1/3$, $I = \{2\}$

$d_3 = [0 \quad 0]$. The inner product of $\nabla f(x_3)$ and d_3 is zero. STOP. Vector $[0 \quad 1/3]$ is an optimal solution.

d. Consider the problem in which function $f(x_1, x_2) = x_1 - 2x_2$ is minimized over the rectangle given in part c. Let $x_k = [0 \quad 1-1/k]$, $k = 1, 2, \ldots$. For each iterate x_k the direction - finding map $D(x)$ defined in part (a) gives $D(x_k) = d_k = [-1 \quad 1]$. Thus we have $\{x_k, d_k\} \rightarrow (\bar{x}, \bar{d})$ where $\bar{x}$

$= [0 \quad 1]$ and $\overline{d} = [-1 \quad 1]$. However, $D(\overline{x}) = [-1 \quad 0] \neq [-1 \quad 1]$. This means that $D(x)$ is not closed at $\overline{x}$.

For the direction map $D(x)$ described in part (b) we obtain

$$D(x_k) = d_k = \frac{1}{\sqrt{5}}[-1 \quad 2], \quad \{x_k, d_k\} \rightarrow (\overline{x}, \overline{d}) \text{ where } \overline{x} = [0 \quad 1] \text{ and } \overline{d} = \frac{1}{\sqrt{5}}[-1 \quad 2],$$

$D(\overline{x}) = [-1 \quad 0] \neq \overline{d}$. Hence, also in this case, the direction finding map is not closed.

10.17. Let $Q(d; \overline{x}) = \frac{1}{2}d^t H(\overline{x})d + \nabla f(\overline{x})^t d$.

a. Second order approximation problem, (QA), is as follows:

$$\text{minimize } Q(d; \overline{x})$$

subject to
$$d_j \geq 0, j \in J_0$$

$$-1 \leq d_j \leq 1 \quad \text{for } j = 1, ..., n \qquad (QA)$$

$$Ad = 0$$

Let d^* denote an optimal solution to the problem (QA).

b. In the problem (QA) a strictly convex function is minimized over a nonempty polyhedron. Therefore, the KKT conditions are both necessary and sufficient for optimality. If $d^* = 0$, then there exist scalars $u_j \geq 0, j \in J_0$, and a vector v such that

$$\nabla Q(0; \overline{x}) - \sum_{j \in J_0} u_j e_j + A^t v = 0,$$

where e_j is the jth unit vector in R^n.

Notice that $\nabla Q(d; \overline{x}) = H(\overline{x})d + \nabla f(\overline{x})$, which yields $\nabla Q(0; \overline{x}) = \nabla f(\overline{x})$. Therefore, if $d^* = 0$ solves the problem (QA), then there exist scalars $u_j \geq 0, j \in J_0$, and a vector v such that

$$\nabla f(\overline{x}) - \sum_{j \in J_0} u_j e_j + A^t v = 0.$$

This implies that $\overline{x}$ is a KKT point for the original problem.

c. Suppose that $d^* \neq 0$. Then $Q(d^*; \overline{x}) < 0$, since $d = 0$ is a feasible solution. Furthermore, since $H(\overline{x})$ is a positive definite matrix, we necessarily have $\nabla f(\overline{x})d^* < 0$. Thus, d^* is an improving direction of $f(\overline{x})$ at $\overline{x}$. $\square$

10.19. The KKT conditions are:

$$4x_1 - 2x_2 + 4x_1u_1 + u_2 - u_3 \quad = 4$$

$$-2x_1 + 4x_2 \quad - u_1 \quad + 5u_2 \quad - u_4 = 6$$

$$u_1(2x_1^2 - x_2) = 0, \; u_2(x_1 + 5x_2 - 5) = 0$$

$$u_3x_1 = 0, \; u_4x_1 = 0$$

$$x_1 \geq 0, \; x_2 \geq 0, \; u_i \geq 0 \text{ for } i = 1, 2, 3, 4.$$

The above KKT system has a unique solution:

$$\overline{x}_1 = (\sqrt{201} - 1)/20$$

$$\overline{x}_2 = (101 - \sqrt{201})/100$$

$$\overline{u}_1 = 0.82243058, \; \overline{u}_2 = 0.93345463, \; \overline{u}_3 = \overline{u}_4 = 0.$$

By Theorem 9.3.1, a suitable value for μ is any real number such that $\mu \geq 0.93345463$.

The Hessian H of the objective function $f(x)$ is $H = \begin{bmatrix} 4 & -2 \\ -2 & 4 \end{bmatrix}$. Its eigenvalues are $\lambda_1 = 6$, and $\lambda_2 = 2$. Vectors $[-1 \; 1]^t$ and $[1 \; 1]^t$ are eigenvectors corresponding to λ_1 and λ_2, respectively.

Unconstrained minimum of $f(x)$ can be found by solving the system $\nabla f(x) = 0$. For the problem in Example 10.3.2 this system is:

$$4x_1 - 2x_2 = 4$$

$$-2x_1 + 4x_2 = 6.$$

The unique solution to the above system is $x_1^* = 7/3$, $x_2^* = 8/3$.

Successive iterations of Algorithm PSLP (note that constant terms $f(x_k) - \nabla f(x_k)^t x_k$ are not included in the objective function of problem $LP(x_k, \Delta_k)$):

Iteration 2.

$x_2 = (0.5, 0.9)$, $\Delta_2 = (1, 1)$,

$LP(x_2, \Delta_2):$ minimize $-3.8x_1 - 3.4x_2 + 10\max(0, -0.5 + 2x_1 - x_2)$

subject to $x_1 + 5x_2 \leq 5$

$$0 \leq x_1 \leq 1.5, \quad 0 \leq x_2 \leq 1.9.$$

Optimal solution to LP(x_2, Δ_2) is $x_1 = 15/22$, $x_2 = 19/22$.

$\Delta F_{E_2} = -0.13868$, and $\Delta F_{EL_2} = 0.5672$, $R_2 < 0$.

We need to shrink Δ_2 to (0.5 , 0.5) and repeat this step.

LP(x_2, Δ_2) :   minimize $-3.8x_1 - 3.4x_2 + 10\max(0, -0.5 + 2x_1 - x_2)$

                subject to $x_1 + 5x_2 \leq 5$

$$0 \leq x_1 \leq 1, \quad 0.4 \leq x_2 \leq 1.4.$$

Optimal solution to LP(x_2, Δ_2) is $x_1 = 15/22$, $x_2 = 19/22$.

$\Delta F_{E_2} = -0.13868$, and $\Delta F_{EL_2} = 0.5672$, $R_2 < 0$.

We need to shrink Δ_2 to (0.25 , 0.25) and repeat this step.

LP(x_2, Δ_2) :   minimize $-3.8x_1 - 3.4x_2 + 10\max(0, -0.5 + 2x_1 - x_2)$

                subject to $x_1 + 5x_2 \leq 5$

$$0.25 \leq x_1 \leq 0.75, \quad 0.65 \leq x_2 \leq 1.15.$$

Optimal solution to LP(x_2, Δ_2) is $x_1 = 15/22$, $x_2 = 19/22$.

$\Delta F_{E_2} = -0.13868$, and $\Delta F_{EL_2} = 0.5672$, $R_2 < 0$.

We need to shrink Δ_2 to (0.125 , 0.125) and repeat this step.

LP(x_2, Δ_2) :   minimize $-3.8x_1 - 3.4x_2 + 10\max(0, -0.5 + 2x_1 - x_2)$

                subject to $x_1 + 5x_2 \leq 5$

$$0.375 \leq x_1 \leq 0.625, \quad 0.785 \leq x_2 \leq 1.025.$$

Optimal solution to LP(x_2, Δ_2) is $x_1 = 0.625$, $x_2 = 0.875$.

$\Delta F_{E_2} = 0.51325$, and $\Delta F_{EL_2} = 0.39$, $R_2 = 1.1316 > \rho_2$. Amplify the trust region by the factor of 2.

Iteration 3.

$x_3 = (0.625, 0.875)$, $\Delta_3 = (0.25, 0.25)$.

LP(x_3, Δ_3) : minimize $-3.25x_1 - 3.75x_2 + 10\max(0, -0.78125 + 2.5x_1 - x_2)$.

                subject to $x_1 + 5x_2 \leq 5$

$$0.375 \le x_1 \le 0.875, \quad 0.625 \le x_2 \le 1.125.$$

Optimal solution to LP(x_3, Δ_3) is $x_1 = 0.6597$, $x_2 = 0.86806$.

$\Delta F_{E_3} = 0.060282056$, and $\Delta F_{EL_3} = 0.8675$, $R_2 = 0.6949$. Retain Δ_3.

Iteration 4.

$x_4 = (0.6597, \ 0.86806)$, $\Delta_4 = (0.25, 0.25)$.

LP(x_4, Δ_4) :

minimize $-3.09732x_1 - 3.84716x_2 + 10\max(0, -0.87040818 + 2.6388x_1 - x_2)$.

$\qquad$ subject to $\qquad x_1 + 5x_2 \le 5$

$$0.4097 \le x_1 \le 0.9097, \quad 0.61806 \le x_2 \le 1.11806.$$

Optimal solution to LP(x_4, Δ_4) is $x_1 = 0.65887$, $x_2 = 0.86823$.

$\Delta F_{E_4} = 0.021547944$, and $\Delta F_{EL_4} = 0.022137689$, $R_2 = 0.97336$. Amplify Δ_4.

Iteration 5.

$x_5 = (0.65887, \ 0.86823)$, $\Delta_5 = (0.5, 0.5)$.

LP(x_5, Δ_5) :

minimize $-3.10098x_1 - 3.84482x_2 + 10\max(0, -0.868219353 + 2.63548x_1 - x_2)$.

$\qquad$ subject to $\qquad x_1 + 5x_2 \le 5$

$$0.15887 \le x_1 \le 1.15887, \quad 0.36823 \le x_2 \le 1.366823.$$

Optimal solution to LP(x_5, Δ_5) is $x_1 = 0.65887$, $x_2 = 0.86826$.

$\Delta F_{E_5} = 0.0$. STOP. $(x_1, x_2) = (0.65887, \ 0.86826)$ is close enough to the KKT point.

10.30. Let $F(d) = ||-\nabla f(x) - d||^2$. Since the Euclidian norm is used, we readily have

$F(d) = d^t d + 2\nabla f(x)^t d + \nabla f(x)^t \nabla f(x)$. Let $\overline{d}$ denote an optimal solution to the problem

$$\min\{ F(d) : A_1 d = 0\}.$$

a. Function $F(d)$ is strictly convex, while the system of constraints $A_1 d = 0$ is linear and

consistent. Therefore, the KKT conditions are both necessary and sufficient. A vector $\overline{d}$ is a KKT

point for the problem $\min\{ F(d) : A_1 d = 0\}$ if $\overline{d} = -\nabla f(x) + A_1^t u$ and $A_1 \overline{d} = 0$.

If $\overline{d}$ solves $\min\{\ F(d) : A_1 d = 0\}$, then it must be a KKT point, that is:

1. It is in the nullspace, $N(A_1)$ of A_1.

2. It is a sum of $A_1^t u$, which is in the orthogonal complement of the nullspace of A_1, and $-\nabla f(x)$.

From linear algebra, we can therefore claim that $\overline{d}$ is the projection vector of $-\nabla f(x)$ onto the nullspace of A_1. If so, out of all vectors in $N(A_1)$, $\overline{d}$ is the closest to $-\nabla f(x)$.

If $\overline{d}$ is the projection vector of $-\nabla f(x)$ onto $N(A_1)$, then

1. $\overline{d}$ must be a vector in $N(A_1)$, that is $A_1 \overline{d} = 0$

2. there exists a unique vector $-z$ in the orthogonal complement of $N(A_1)$ such that $\overline{d} - z = -\nabla f(x)$.

That is, there exists a vector u such that $A_1^t u = z$, which further yields the existence of a solution to the system $A_1 \overline{d} = 0$, $-\nabla f(x) = \overline{d} - A_1^t u$. Thus, $\overline{d}$ is a KKT point. $\square$

b. By premultiplying equation $d = -\nabla f(x) + A_1^t u$ by A_1, and noting that $A_1 d = 0$, we obtain $-A_1 \nabla f(x) + A_1 A_1^t u = 0$. If A_1^t is of full rank, then $u = (A_1 A_1^t)^{-1} A_1 \nabla f(x)$, so that

$$d = [\ -I + A_1^t (A_1 A_1^t)^{-1} A_1] \nabla f(x).$$

(One can observe that by the derivation in part (a), we directly have $d = -P\nabla f(x)$, where $P = I - A_1^t(A_1 A_1^t)^{-1} A_1$ is the projection matrix onto the nullspace of A_1.) $\square$

c. $\nabla f(x) = [1 \quad -2 \quad 3]^t$, $A_1 = \begin{bmatrix} 1 & 2 & -3 \\ 2 & 1 & 1 \end{bmatrix}$, and $d = \frac{1}{83}[\ -50 \quad 70 \quad 30]^t$.

10.37. a. Let $M^t = [\ A^t \ -E^t]$, where E^t is an $nx(n-m)$ submatrix of I_n (columns of I_n corresponding to nonbasic variables). By assumption, A is an mxn matrix whose rank is m. Furthermore, $rank(E^t) = n-m$, and so by construction, M^t is an nxn matrix of full rank. This implies that matrix $M^t M$ is invertible. The projection matrix P onto the (left) nullspace of the gradients of binding constraints is then given as $P = I - M^t(MM^t)^{-1}M$, and the direction vector d is then given as $d = -Pc$. Notice that $Md = -MPc$, which by the equation for P gives $Md = -Mc + MM^t(MM^t)^{-1}Mc$, thus resulting in $Md = 0$. Therefore, d must be the zero vector since M is nonsingular.   □

b. Let $u^t = [\, u_0^t \ \ u_1^t]$, where u_0 and u_1 are mx1 and (n−m)x1 vectors, respectively. Vector u_0 is associated with the equality constraints $Ax = b$, while vector u_1 is associated with m-n nonnegativity constraints $x_j \geq 0$. Equation $u = - (MM^t)^{-1}Mc$ can be rewritten as $MM^t u = -Mc$, which by the structure of matrix M and vector u gives the following system

$$AA^t u_0 - AE^t u_1 = -Ac$$

$$-EA^t u_0 + EE^t u_1 = Ec.$$

If $A = [\, B \ N]$, where B is an mxm invertible matrix, and $c^t = [c_B^t \ \ c_N^t]$ then

$$AA^t = BB^t + NN^t, \quad AE^t = N, \quad EE^t = I_{n-m} \ \text{ and } \ Ec = c_N.$$

Therefore, we can rewrite our system of equations as

$$BB^t u_0 + NN^t u_0 - Nu_1 = -Bc_B - Nc_N$$

$$-N^t u_0 + u_1 = c_N.$$

By premultiplying the second subsystem by matrix N, and next adding the resulting equation to the first one, we obtain $BB^t u_0 = -Bc_B$. That is, $u_0 = -(B^t)^{-1}c_B$, which further gives $u_1 = c_N - N^t(B^{-1})^t c_B$. This means that the jth entry of vector u_1 is simply the value of $c_j - z_j$ used in the simplex method. Thus, the most negative u_j associated with the constraint $x_j \geq 0$ is the most negative value of $c_j - z_j$ in the simplex method.

c. Given that $d' = P'c$, we have $x' = x + \lambda d'$, , where $\lambda \geq 0$, so that we now need to show that d'
$$= \begin{bmatrix} -B^{-1}a_j \\ e_j \end{bmatrix},$$
where j is the index of entering variable in the simplex method. By construction,

$P' = I - M'^t(M'M'^t)^{-1}M'$, where $M' = \begin{bmatrix} A \\ -E' \end{bmatrix}$, and where E' is formed from E by deleting e_j. Let us rewrite matrix A using three blocks: matrix B, column a_j, and matrix N' (notice that $N = [\, a_j \ N]$). This allows us to rewrite matrix M' in the following way:

$$M' = \begin{bmatrix} B & a_j & N' \\ 0 & 0 & -I \end{bmatrix}, \text{ where I is of order } n-m-1.$$

Further, let $d'^t = [d_B^t \quad d_j \quad d_{N'}^t]$. Since $M'd' = 0$, we obtain

$$Bd_B + a_j d_j + N' d_{N'} = 0 \text{ and } d_{N'} = 0.$$

This yields $d_B = -B^{-1} a_j d_j$, d_j - unrestricted and $d_{N'} = 0$. Thus $d' = \begin{bmatrix} -B^{-1} a_j \\ e_j \end{bmatrix}$. □

10.42. a. Results of the gradient projection method:

Iteration 1.

$$x_1 = [\, 0 \quad 0 \quad 2\,]^t, \quad A_1 = \begin{bmatrix} -1 & 0 & 0 \\ 0 & -1 & 0 \end{bmatrix}, \quad M = \begin{bmatrix} -1 & 0 & 0 \\ 0 & -1 & 0 \\ 1 & 1 & 1 \end{bmatrix}, \quad P = 0_{3x3},$$

$w = [\, -6 \quad -14 \quad 0\,]^t$. Drop u_2.

$$A_1 = [\, -1 \quad 0 \quad 0\,], \quad M = \begin{bmatrix} -1 & 0 & 0 \\ 1 & 1 & 1 \end{bmatrix}, \quad P = \frac{1}{2} \begin{bmatrix} 0 & 0 & 0 \\ 0 & 1 & -1 \\ 0 & -1 & 1 \end{bmatrix},$$

$d = [\, 0 \quad 7 \quad -7\,]^t$.

$\lambda = 3/14$

Iteration 2.

$$x_2 = [\, 0 \quad 3/2 \quad 1/2\,]^t, \quad M = \begin{bmatrix} -1 & 2 & 0 \\ -1 & 0 & 0 \\ 1 & 1 & 1 \end{bmatrix}, \quad P = 0_{3x3},$$

$w = [\, 4 \quad -8.5 \quad 0\,]^t$. Delete row 2.

$$M = \begin{bmatrix} -1 & 2 & 0 \\ 1 & 1 & 1 \end{bmatrix}, \quad P = \frac{1}{14} \begin{bmatrix} 4 & 2 & -6 \\ 2 & 1 & -3 \\ -6 & -3 & 9 \end{bmatrix}, \quad d = \frac{1}{14} [\, 34 \quad 17 \quad -51\,]^t$$

$\lambda = 7/51$.

Iteration 3.

$$x_3 = \frac{1}{3} [\, 1 \quad 5 \quad 0\,]^t, \quad M = \begin{bmatrix} -1 & 2 & 0 \\ 0 & 0 & -1 \\ 1 & 1 & 1 \end{bmatrix}, \quad P = 0_{3x3},$$

$w = \frac{1}{9} [10 \quad 43 \quad 43]^t \geq 0$. Stop; x_3 is a KKT point for this problem.

b. Results of the reduced gradient method:

$x_1 = [0 \quad 0 \quad 0 \quad 2 \quad 3]^t$

Iteration 1.

	x_1	x_2	x_3	x_4
Solution x_1	0	0	2	3
$\nabla f(x_1)$	-6	-14	0	0
$\nabla_B f(x_1) = \begin{bmatrix} 0 \\ 0 \end{bmatrix}$	1	1	1	0
	-1	2	0	1
r	-6	-14	0	0
d	6	14	-20	-22

$\lambda_1 = 1/10$.

Iteration 2.

	x_1	x_2	x_3	x_4
Solution x_2	0.6	1.4	0	0.8
$\nabla f(x_2)$	-3.4	-7.8	0	0
$\nabla_B f(x_2) = \begin{bmatrix} -7.8 \\ 0 \end{bmatrix}$	1	1	1	0
	-3	0	-2	1
r	4.4	0	7.8	0
d	-2.64	2.64	0	-7.92

$\lambda_2 = 10/99$

Iteration 3.

	x_1	x_2	x_3	x_4
Solution x_3	1/3	5/3	0	0
$\nabla f(x_3)$	−11/3	−7	0	0
$\nabla_B f(x_3) = \begin{bmatrix} -7 \\ -11/3 \end{bmatrix}$	0	1	1/3	1/3
	1	0	2/3	−1/3
r	0	0	43/9	10/9
d	0	0	0	0

Stop; x_3 is a KKT point for this problem.

c. Results of the convex simplex method:

$x_1 = \begin{bmatrix} 0 & 0 & 0 & 2 & 3 \end{bmatrix}^t$

Iteration 1.

	x_1	x_2	x_3	x_4
Solution x_1	0	0	2	3
$\nabla f(x_1)$	−6	−14	0	0
$\nabla_B f(x_1) = \begin{bmatrix} 0 \\ 0 \end{bmatrix}$	1	1	1	0
	−1	2	0	1
r	−6	−14	0	0

$\alpha = 14,\ \beta = 0;\ \alpha > \beta;\ \nu = 2;\ d = \begin{bmatrix} 0 & 1 & -1 & -2 \end{bmatrix}^t;$
$\lambda_{max} = \min\ \{\ 2,\ 3/2\} = 3/2;\ \lambda_1 = \min\ \{\ 3/2,\ 7/6\ \} = 3/2.$

Iteration 2.

	x_1	x_2	x_3	x_4
Solution x_2	0	3/2	1/2	0
$\nabla f(x_2)$	−9/2	−8	0	0
$\nabla_B f(x_2) = \begin{bmatrix} 0 \\ -8 \end{bmatrix}$	3/2	0	1	1/2
	−1/2	1	0	1/2
r	−17/2	0	0	4

$\alpha = 17/2,\ \beta = 0;\ \alpha > \beta;\ \nu = 1;\ d = [\ 1\quad 1/2\quad -3/2\quad 0\ ]^t$

$\lambda_{max} = 1/3;\ \lambda_2 = \min\ \{\ 1/3,\ \ 17/7\ \} = 1/3.$

Iteration 3.

	x_1	x_2	x_3	x_4
Solution x_3	1/3	5/3	0	0
$\nabla f(x_3)$	$-11/3$	-7	0	0
$\nabla_B f(x_3) = \begin{bmatrix} -7 \\ -11/3 \end{bmatrix}$	0	1	1/3	1/3
	1	0	2/3	$-1/3$
r	0	0	43/9	10/9

$\alpha = 0,\ \beta = 0.$ Stop; x_3 is a KKT point for this problem.

d. Define

$X = \{\ x \in R^3:\ -x_1 + 2x_2 \le 3,\ x_1 \ge 0,\ x_2 \ge 0,\ x_3 \ge 0\}$

$h(x) = x_1 + x_2 + x_3 - 2.$

Let $\rho_0 = 10^{-6}$, $\rho_1 = 0.25$, $\rho_2 = 0.75$, and $\beta = 0.5.$

Furthermore, let $x_1 = [\ 0\quad 0\quad 3\ ]^t$, $\Delta_1 = [\ 1\quad 1\quad 1\ ]^t$, $\Delta_{LB} = \rho_0[\ 1\quad 1\quad 1\ ]^t$, and $\mu = 10.$

Iteration 1.

Step 1.

Solve the linear program $LP(x_1,\ \Delta_1)$:

minimize $\qquad -6d_1 - 14d_2 + 10(z^+ + z^-)$

subject to $\qquad d_1 + d_2 + d_3 - z^+ + z^- = 0$

$\qquad\qquad -d_1 + 2d_2 \le 3$

$\qquad\qquad 0 \le d_1 \le 1,\ 0 \le d_2 \le 1,\ -2 \le d_3 \le 1,\ z^+ \ge 0,\ z^- \ge 0.$

Optimal solution is:

$$d_1 = 1,\ d_2 = 1,\ d_3 = -2,\ z^+ = \ z^- = 0,$$

therefore, $d_1 = [\ 1\quad 1\quad -2\ ]^t.$

$\Delta F_{EL_1} = 20,\ \Delta F_{E_1} = 16,$ hence $R_1 = 0.8 > \rho_0.$

Step 2.

$x_2 = [\,1 \quad 1 \quad 1\,]^t.$

$R_1 = 0.8 > \rho_2 = 0.75$, therefore we need to amplify the trust region; $\Delta_2 = [2 \quad 2 \quad 2]^t.$

Iteration 2.

Step 1.

Solve the linear program LP(x_2, Δ_2):

minimize $\qquad -3d_1 - 9d_2 + 10(z^+ + z^-)$

subject to $\qquad d_1 + d_2 + d_3 - z^+ + z^- = 0$

$\qquad\qquad -d_1 + 2d_2 \le 2$

$\qquad\qquad -1 \le d_1 \le 2,\; -1 \le d_2 \le 2,\; 0 \le d_3 \le 2,\; z^+ \ge 0,\; z^- \ge 0.$

Optimal solution is:

$$d_1 = -2/3,\; d_2 = 2/3,\; d_3 = z^+ = z^- = 0,$$

therefore, $d_2 = 1/3\,[\,-1 \quad 1 \quad 0\,].$

$\Delta F_{EL_2} = 4,\; \Delta F_{E_2} = 10/3$, hence $R_1 = 5/6 > \rho_0.$

Step 2.

$x_3 = [\,1/3 \quad 5/3 \quad 0\,]^t.$

$R_2 = 5/6 > \rho_2 = 0.75$. Therefore, we need to amplify the trust region; $\Delta_3 = [4 \quad 4 \quad 4]^t.$

Iteration 3.

Step 1.

Solve the linear program LP(x_3, Δ_3):

minimize $\qquad -\frac{11}{3}d_1 - 7d_2 + 10(z^+ + z^-)$

subject to $\qquad d_1 + d_2 + d_3 - z^+ + z^- = 0$

$\qquad\qquad -d_1 + 2d_2 \le 0$

$\qquad\qquad -1/3 \le d_1 \le 4,\; -5/3 \le d_2 \le 4,\; 0 \le d_3 \le 4,\; z^+ \ge 0,\; z^- \ge 0.$

Optimal solution is:

$$d_1 = d_2 = d_3 = z^+ = z^- = 0,$$

therefore, $d_3 = [\,0 \quad 0 \quad 0\,]^t$. Stop. $x = [\,1/3 \quad 5/3 \quad 0\,]^t$ is an optimal solution.

e. For convenience, let us rewrite the problem in an equivalent way using only two variables x_1 and x_2:   minimize $\{f(x): g_i(x) \leq 0 \text{ for } i = 1, ..., 4\}$,

where
$$f(x) = x_1^2 + x_1 x_2 + 2x_2^2 - 6x_1 - 14x_2,$$

$$g_1(x) = x_1 + x_2 - 2$$

$$g_2(x) = -x_1 + 2x_2 - 3$$

$$g_3(x) = -x_1, \text{ and } g_4(x) = -x_2.$$

Start with $x_1 = [\,0 \quad 0\,]^t$ and $u_1 = [\,0 \quad 0 \quad 0 \quad 0\,]^t$. Let $B_1 = \nabla^2 L(x) = \begin{bmatrix} 2 & 1 \\ 1 & 4 \end{bmatrix}$.

Iteration 1.

Solve (QP):

minimize $d_1^2 + d_1 d_2 + 2d_2^2 - 6d_1 - 14d_2$

subject to $d_1 + d_2 \leq 2$

$$-d_1 + 2d_2 \leq 3$$

$$d_1 \geq 0, d_2 \geq 0.$$

Optimal solution to the foregoing (QP) is $d_1 = [\,1/3 \quad 5/3\,]^t$. Only the first two constraints are binding at d_1, hence we set $u_3 = u_4 = 0$, and find u_1 and u_2 from the KKT system

$$2d_1 + d_2 - 6 + u_1 - u_2 = 0$$

$$d_1 + 4d_2 - 14 + u_1 + 2u_2 = 0.$$

Given that $d_1 = [\,1/3 \quad 5/3\,]^t$, we obtain $u_1 = 43/9$ and $u_2 = 10/9$. Next we need to determine step length λ by minimizing $F_E(x_1 + \lambda d_1)$ over $\lambda \geq 0$. Let $\mu = 10$. Simple algebra leads to the following expression for $F_E(x_1 + \lambda d_1)$:

$$F_E(x_1 + \lambda d_1) = \frac{56}{9}\lambda^2 - \frac{20}{3}\lambda + 10\Big(\max(0, 2\lambda - 2) + \max(0, -3\lambda - 3)$$
$$+ \max(0, -\tfrac{\lambda}{3}) + \max(0, -\tfrac{5\lambda}{3})\Big).$$

The minimum value of $F_E(x_1 + \lambda d_1)$ over $\lambda \geq 0$ is $-4/3$, and is attained at $\lambda = 1$.

Therefore, $x_2 = [\,1/3 \quad 5/3\,]^t$, $u_2 = [\,43/9 \quad 10/9 \quad 0 \quad 0\,]^t$.

Iteration 2.

With $B_2 = B_1$ we need to solve (QP):

minimize $\quad\quad\quad d_1^2 + d_1d_2 + 2d_2^2 - 6d_1 - 14d_2$

subject to $\quad\quad\quad d_1 + d_2 \le 0$

$$-d_1 + 2d_2 \le 0$$

$$d_1 \ge -1/3, \ d_2 \ge -5/3.$$

The optimal solution to this problem is $d_2 = [\ 0 \quad 0\ ]^t$. Again, only the first two constraint are binding, hence Lagrange multipliers u_3 and u_4 are both equal to zero. Values of u_1 and u_2 are determined via the KKT system:

$$2d_1 + d_2 - 6 + u_1 - u_2 = 0$$

$$d_1 + 4d_2 - 14 + u_1 + 2u_2 = 0.$$

Given that $d_2 = [\ 0 \quad 0\ ]^t$, we obtain $u_1 = 26/3$ and $u_2 = 8/3$, thus $u_3 = [\ 26/3 \quad 8/3 \quad 0 \quad 0]^t$.

Since $d_2 = 0$, stop. Vector $x_2 = [\ 1/3 \quad 5/3\ ]^t$ is a KKT point (in this case , it is an optimal solution), and $u_3 = [26/3 \quad 8/3 \quad 0 \quad 0]^t$ is the corresponding vector of Lagrange multipliers.

10.43. Add slack variables x_3 and x_4 to the first two inequalities.

Start with $x_1 = [\ 0 \quad 0 \quad 0 \quad 2 \quad 3]^t$. $I = \{3, 4\}$

Iteration 1.

	x_1	x_2	x_3	x_4
Solution x_1	0	0	6	3
$\nabla f(x_1)$	1	-2	0	0
$\nabla_B f(x_1) = \begin{bmatrix} 0 \\ 0 \end{bmatrix}$	1	2	1	0
	-1	2	0	1
r	1	-2	0	0

$\alpha = 2, \beta = 0; \alpha > \beta; \nu = 2; \; d = [\,0 \quad 1 \quad -2 \quad -2\,]^t;$

$\lambda_{max} = \min\{\,3, 3/2\,\} = 3/2; \lambda_1 = \min\{\,3/2, \; 1/\sqrt{3}\,\} = 1/\sqrt{3}.$

Iteration 2. $I = \{3, 4\}.$

	x_1	x_2	x_3	x_4
Solution x_2	0	$1/\sqrt{3}$	$6\text{-}2/\sqrt{3}$	$3\text{-}2/\sqrt{3}$
$\nabla f(x_2)$	1	0	0	0
$\nabla_B f(x_2) = \begin{bmatrix} 0 \\ 0 \end{bmatrix}$	1	2	1	0
	-1	2	0	1
r	1	0	0	0

$\alpha = 0, \beta = 0;$ STOP. $\overline{x}_1 = 0, \overline{x}_2 = 1/\sqrt{3}$ is a KKT point.

The solution $\overline{x}_1 = 0, \overline{x}_2 = 1/\sqrt{3}$ is the unique global optimum.

10.50. Since $Bx_B + Nx_N = b$, we obtain $x_B = B^{-1}b - B^{-1}Nx_N$. To guarantee that all variables take on nonnegative values only, we need to require that $B^{-1}b - B^{-1}Nx_N \geq 0$ and $x_N \geq 0$. Furthermore, by substituting $B^{-1}b - B^{-1}Nx_N$ for x_B into the objective function we obtain an equivalent problem $P(x_N)$ in the nonbasic variable space.

a. At the current solution x_N the binding constraints are $x_N \geq 0$. By rules for differentiating we obtain

$$\nabla F(x_N)^t = -\nabla_B f(B^{-1}b - B^{-1}Nx_N, x_N)^t B^{-1}N + \nabla_N f(B^{-1}b - B^{-1}Nx_N, x_N)^t.$$

From the above equation it follows that $\nabla F(x_N) = r_N$ in the reduced gradient method.

b. The KKT system for $P(x_N)$ is:

$$-(B^{-1}N)^t \nabla_B f(B^{-1}b - B^{-1}Nx_N, x_N) + \nabla_N f(B^{-1}b - B^{-1}Nx_N, x_N) + (B^{-1}N)^t u - w = 0$$

$$B^{-1}b - B^{-1}Nx_N \geq 0,$$

$$x_N \geq 0, u \geq 0, w \geq 0$$

$$u^t(B^{-1}b - B^{-1}Nx_N) = 0, \quad x_N^t w = 0.$$

Since $\bar{x}_B = B^{-1}b - B^{-1}N\bar{x}_N > 0$, we necessarily have $\bar{u} = 0$. Therefore, at $\bar{x}_N$ we have

$\bar{w} = \nabla_N f(B^{-1}b - B^{-1}N\bar{x}_N, \bar{x}_N) - (B^{-1}N)^t \nabla_B f(B^{-1}b - B^{-1}N\bar{x}_N, \bar{x}_N)$, so that the KKT system

reduces to the following:

$$\nabla_N f(B^{-1}b - B^{-1}N\bar{x}_N, \bar{x}_N) - (B^{-1}N)^t \nabla_B f(B^{-1}b - B^{-1}N\bar{x}_N, \bar{x}_N) \geq 0$$

$$\bar{x}_N^t \left(\nabla_N f(B^{-1}b - B^{-1}N\bar{x}_N, \bar{x}_N) - (B^{-1}N)^t \nabla_B f(B^{-1}b - B^{-1}N\bar{x}_N, \bar{x}_N) \right) = 0,$$

or shortly to:

$$r_N \geq 0, \quad x_N^t r_N = 0, \text{ where}$$

$$r_N = \nabla_N f(B^{-1}b - B^{-1}N\bar{x}_N, \bar{x}_N) - (B^{-1}N)^t \nabla_B f(B^{-1}b - B^{-1}N\bar{x}_N, \bar{x}_N) \geq 0.$$

The foregoing necessary and sufficient conditions for $\bar{x}_N$ to be a KKT point for $P(x_N)$ are identical to the stopping rule used in the reduced gradient method (Theorem 10.6.1), which in fact gives necessary and sufficient conditions for $(\bar{x}_B, \bar{x}_N)$ to be a KKT point for the original problem.

ANSWERS TO SELECTED EXERCISES

IN CHAPTER 11

11.3. a.
$$-u + A^t v = -c$$

$$Ax = b$$

$$u^t x = 0, \ x \geq 0, \ u \geq 0.$$

b. The KKT system for the problem given in part (b) is:

$$u_1 - u_2 - u_3 = 1$$

$$u_1 + u_2 \qquad - u_4 = 3$$

$$x_1 + x_2 + y_1 \qquad = 6$$

$$-x_1 + x_2 \qquad + y_2 = 4,$$

$$x_1 u_3 = 0, \ x_2 u_4 = 0, \ u_1 y_1 = 0, \ u_2 y_2 = 0$$

$$x_1 \geq 0, \ x_2 \geq 0, \ y_1 \geq 0, \ y_2 \geq 0, \ u_i \geq 0 \text{ for } i = 1, 2, 3, 4.$$

Let $w = [\, u_3 \ u_4 \ y_1 \ y_2\,]^t$, $z = [x_1 \ x_2 \ u_1 \ u_2]^t$, $q = [\,-1 \quad 3 \quad 6 \quad 4\,]^t$, and

$$M = \begin{bmatrix} 0 & 0 & 1 & -1 \\ 0 & 0 & 1 & 1 \\ -1 & -1 & 0 & 0 \\ 1 & -1 & 0 & 0 \end{bmatrix}.$$

Then the KKT system can be rewritten as a linear complementarity problem: $w - Mz = q$, $w \geq 0$,

$z \geq 0$, $w^t z = 0$.

Results of the complementary pivoting algorithm:

w_1	w_2	w_3	w_4	z_1	z_2	z_3	z_4	z_0	RHS
1	0	0	0	0	0	-1	1	-1	-1
0	1	0	0	0	0	-1	-1	-1	-3
0	0	1	0	1	1	0	0	-1	6
0	0	0	1	-1	1	0	0	-1	4
1	-1	0	0	0	0	0	2	0	2
0	-1	0	0	0	0	1	1	1	3
0	-1	1	0	1	1	1	1	0	9
0	-1	0	1	-1	1	1	1	0	7
1	-1	0	0	0	0	0	2	0	2
0	-1	0	0	0	0	1	1	1	3
0	1	1	-1	2	0	0	0	0	2
0	-1	0	1	-1	1	1	1	0	7
0.5	-0.5	0	0	0	0	0	1	0	1
-0.5	-0.5	0	0	0	0	1	0	1	2
0	1	1	-1	2	0	0	0	0	2
-0.5	-0.5	0	1	-1	1	1	0	0	6
0.5	-0.5	0	0	0	0	0	1	0	1
-0.5	-0.5	0	0	0	0	1	0	1	2
0	0.5	0.5	-0.5	1	0	0	0	0	1
-0.5	0	0.5	0.5	0	1	1	0	0	7
0.5	-0.5	0	0	0	0	0	1	0	1
-0.5	-0.5	0	0	0	0	1	0	1	2
0	0.5	0.5	-0.5	1	0	0	0	0	1
0	0.5	0.5	0.5	0	1	0	0	-1	5

Algorithm stops with $z_0 = 0$, hence a solution to the linear complementarity problem has been obtained: $x_1 = 1$, $x_2 = 5$, $u_1 = 2$, and $u_2 = 1$. All the remaining variables are equal to zero.

11.5. a. Let 1_p denote a px1 vector of ones. An equilibrium pair $(\bar{x}, \bar{y})$ for a bimatrix game with loss matrices A and B can be obtained as a partial solution to the linear complementary problem

$w - Mz = q$, $w \geq 0$, $z \geq 0$, $w^t z = 0$, where $w^t = [\ w_1^t \quad w_2^t \quad s_1 \quad s_2 \quad s_3 \quad s_4\ ]$,

$z^t = [\ x^t \quad y^t \quad v_1 \quad v_2 \quad v_3 \quad v_4\ ]$, $q^t = [\ 0^t \quad 0^t \quad 1 \quad -1 \quad 1 \quad -1]$, and

$$
M = \begin{bmatrix}
0 & A & 1_m & -1_m & 0 & 0 \\
B^t & 0 & 0 & 0 & 1_n & -1_n \\
-1_m^t & 0 & 0 & 0 & 0 & 0 \\
1_m^t & 0 & 0 & 0 & 0 & 0 \\
0 & -1_n^t & 0 & 0 & 0 & 0 \\
0 & 1_n^t & 0 & 0 & 0 & 0
\end{bmatrix}
$$

and where O denotes a zero matrix of appropriate order.

b. For any $z^t = [\ x^t \quad y^t \quad v_1 \quad v_2 \quad v_3 \quad v_4\ ]$ we have $z^t M z = x^t (A + B) y$, hence matrix M is copositive if matrix $A + B$ is nonnegative. However, matrix M is not necessarily copositive plus. Note that $(M + M^t)z = [\ y^t(A^t + B^t) \quad x^t(A + B) \quad 0 \quad 0 \quad 0\ ]$. Hence $(M + M^t)z \neq 0$ if and only if $[\ y^t(A^t + B^t) \quad x^t(A + B)\ ] \neq 0$. Next, consider the following matrix $A + B$:

$A + B = \begin{bmatrix} 2 & 4 \\ 0 & 10 \end{bmatrix}$. Here, for $x^t = [\ 1 \quad 0\ ]$ and $y^t = [\ 0 \quad 1\ ]$, we have $x^t(A + B)y^t = 0$ and

$x^t(A + B) = [\ 2 \quad 4]$. Therefore, $x^t(A + B)y^t = 0$ does not imply that $x^t(A + B) = 0$, which means that matrix M is not necessarily copositive plus. However, for every bimatrix game an equilibrium pair exists. A proof can be found in *Game Theory* by Guillermo Owen (Academic Press, Second Edition, 1982).

c. For the given matrices A and B, the equilibrium pair is $\overline{x} = [0.5 \quad 0.5]^t$ and $\overline{y} = [0.5 \quad 0.5 \quad 0]^t$.

11.14. Let P and PKKT denote the problems

$$\text{minimize} \qquad f(x) = c^t x + \tfrac{1}{2} x^t H x$$

$$\text{subject to} \qquad Ax = b$$

$$x \geq 0,$$

and

$$\text{minimize} \qquad g(x,u,v) = c^t x - b^t u$$

$$\text{subject to} \qquad Ax = b$$

$$Hx + A^t u - v = -c$$

$$v^t x = 0$$

$$x \geq 0, v \geq 0,$$

respectively.

a. From the KKT system formulation for problem P we can assert that (x, u, v) is a feasible solution for problem PKKT if and only if x is a KKT point for problem P. Furthermore, if a triple (x, u, v) is feasible for PKKT, then we necessarily have $u^t Ax = u^t b$, and $x^t Hx + x^t A^t u = -x^t c$, which yields $x^t Hx = -(c^t x + b^t u)$. Therefore, for any such (x, u, v) the objective function $f(x)$ can be rewritten as $c^t x - \tfrac{1}{2}(c^t x + b^t u)$, and further as $\tfrac{1}{2}(c^t x - b^t u)$. This leads to the conclusion that if (x, u, v) is a feasible solution for problem PKKT, then the value of the objective function $g(x,u,v)$ is twice the value of the original objective function $f(x)$. Therefore, an optimal solution for problem PKKT is a KKT point for problem P with the smallest value of the function $f(x)$. $\qquad\qquad\qquad\qquad\qquad\qquad\qquad\qquad\qquad\qquad\square$

If matrix H is positive semidefinite, and $(\overline{x}, \overline{u}, \overline{v})$ is an optimal solution for problem PKKT, then $\overline{x}$ is a global optimal solution for problem P.

b. Evident from part a.

c. Optimal solution for the given problem is $x_1^* = 3.2$, $x_2^* = 0.8$.

11.20.

a. Suppose that the matrix $\begin{bmatrix} H & A^t \\ A & 0 \end{bmatrix}$ is singular. Then there exists a nonzero vector $[x^t \quad y^t]$,

where $x \in R^n$, $y \in R^m$, such that

$$Hx + A^t y = 0$$

$$Ax \qquad = 0.$$

As a result of premultiplying the first equation by x^t, and the second one by y^t we obtain

$$x^t Hx + x^t A^t y = 0$$

$$y^t Ax \qquad\qquad = 0,$$

which necessarily yields $x^t Hx = 0$. This contradicts the assumption that matrix H is positive

definite over the nullspace of A. Therefore, the given matrix is nonsingular. $\qquad\square$

b. Result is evident from part a.

c. KKT system for this problem is

$$Hx + A^t v = -c$$

$$Ax = b.$$

If matrix H is nonsingular, then from the first equation we obtain $x = H^{-1}(c + A^t v)$. To compute

v, substitute this expression for x into the second equation to obtain $AH^{-1}A^t v = -(AH^{-1}c + b)$,

which gives $v = -(AH^{-1}A^t)^{-1}(AH^{-1}c + b)$. Therefore,

$$x = -H^{-1}c + H^{-1}A^t(AH^{-1}A^t)^{-1}(AH^{-1}c + b).$$

11.22. a. Let $x = x_k + d$. Then

$$c^t x + \tfrac{1}{2}x^t Hx = c^t d + \tfrac{1}{2}d^t Hd + 2x_k^t Hd + c^t x_k + \tfrac{1}{2}x_k^t Hx_k,$$

and for each $i \in W_k$

$$A_i^t x - b_i = A_i^t x_k + A_i^t d - b_k = A_i^t d.$$

This shows that constraints in the two problems are equivalent, and their objective functions

differ by a constant term $c^t x_k + \tfrac{1}{2}x_k^t Hx_k$. Therefore, if d_k solves $QP(x_k)$, then $x_k + d_k$ solves the other problem.

b. KKT equations for the problem $QP(x_k)$ are: $c + Hx_k + Hd + \sum\limits_{i \in W_k} A_i v_i = 0$, where v_i are Lagrange multipliers associated with equations $A_i^t d = 0$ for $i \in W_k$. If $d_k = 0$, then v_i^*, $i \in W_k$, solve

$$c + Hx_k + \sum\limits_{i \in E} A_i v_i + \sum\limits_{i \in I_k} A_i v_i = 0.$$

KKT system for QP at x_k is

$$c + Hx_k + \sum\limits_{i \in E} A_i v_i + \sum\limits_{i \in I_k} A_i v_i = 0,$$

$$v_i \geq 0 \text{ and } v_i(A_i^t x_k - b_i) = 0 \text{ for all } i \in I_k.$$

Therefore, if $v_i^* \geq 0$ for all $i \in I_k$, the x_k is a KKT point for QP.

c. Suppose that x_k is a feasible solution. If the direction vector d_k found as an optimal solution for the problem $QP(x_k)$ is not a zero vector, then a move in the direction d_k is made. If $x_k + d_k$ is feasible, then readily the next iterate $x_{k+1} = x_k + d_k$ is a feasible solution. If $x_k + d_k$ is not a feasible solution, then $x_{k+1} = x_k + \alpha_k d_k$, where α_k is a step length computed via the equation given in this exercise. Next, we show that if α_k is computed in this way, then $x_{k+1} = x_k + \alpha_k d_k$ is a feasible solution. Note that $A_i^t x_k = b_i$ for all $i \in W_k$, and $A_i^t d_k = 0$ for all $i \in W_k$ since vector d_k is feasible for the problem $QP(x_k)$. Therefore, $A_i^t(x_k + \alpha d_k) = b_i$ for all $i \in W_k$ and for any $\alpha \geq 0$. This means that all constraints in the working set W_k remain binding at $x_k + \alpha_k d_k$ for any $\alpha \geq 0$. For an $i \notin I_k$, we either have $A_i^t d_k \leq 0$ or $A_i^t d_k > 0$. In the former case constraint i will be satisfied for any $\alpha \geq 0$, since $A_i^t x_k \leq b_i$. Consider now the latter case. From the equation for α_k we have

$$A_i^t(x_k + \alpha_k d_k) = A_i^t x_k + \frac{b_q - A_q^t x_k}{A_q^t d_k} A_i^t d_k.$$

If $i = q$, then readily $A_q^t(x_k + \alpha_k d_k) = b_q$. If $i \neq q$, then since $A_i^t d_k > 0$ and

$0 \leq \dfrac{b_q - A_q^t x_k}{A_q^t d_k} \leq \dfrac{b_i - A_i^t x_k}{A_i^t d_k}$, we obtain $A_i^t(x_k + \alpha_k d_k) \leq b_i$. Thus we have demonstrated that if the algorithm is initiated with a feasible solution x_1, then feasibility is maintained throughout the algorithm.

Next we show that if $d_k \neq 0$, then $f(x_k) \geq f(x_{k+1})$. Notice that $d=0$ is a feasible solution for the problem $QP(x_k)$. Therefore, by optimality of d_k and uniqueness, we have $\nabla f(x_k)^t d_k + \frac{1}{2} d_k^t H d_k < 0$. But $\frac{1}{2} d_k^t H d_k > 0$, hence $\nabla f(x_k)^t d_k < 0$. This shows that d_k is a descent direction at x_k. Moreover, since $f(x)$ is a quadratic function, $f(x_k + \alpha d_k) = f(x_k) + \alpha \nabla f(x_k)^t d_k + \frac{1}{2} \alpha^2 d_k^t H d_k = f(x_k) + \alpha \left(\nabla f(x_k)^t d_k + \frac{1}{2} d_k^t H d_k \right) + \frac{1}{2} \alpha(\alpha - 1) d_k^t H d_k$, and therefore, we have $f(x_k) > f(x_k + \alpha d_k)$ whenever $0 < \alpha \leq 1$ and $d_k \neq 0$ solves $QP(x_k)$. In this algorithm, if a descent direction is found, then α_k is necessarily in the interval $(0, 1]$, hence $f(x_{k+1}) < f(x_k)$. The foregoing results let us assert that the algorithm either verifies that a feasible solution is optimal or else finds a better feasible solution. In the latter case, a change in the working set may be necessary. However, since the number of working sets is finite, the algorithm must terminate with an optimal solution after a finite number of steps.

d. The problem to be solved is:

$$\text{minimize} \ -2x_1 - 6x_2 + x_1^2 - 2x_1 x_2 + 2x_2^2$$
$$\text{subject to} \quad x_1 + x_2 \leq 2$$
$$-x_1 + 2x_2 \leq 2$$
$$x_1 \geq 0, \ x_2 \geq 0.$$

Therefore,

$$A_1 = \begin{bmatrix} 1 \\ 1 \end{bmatrix}, \ A_2 = \begin{bmatrix} -1 \\ 2 \end{bmatrix}, \ A_3 = \begin{bmatrix} -1 \\ 0 \end{bmatrix}, \ A_4 = \begin{bmatrix} 0 \\ -1 \end{bmatrix}, \ c = \begin{bmatrix} -2 \\ -6 \end{bmatrix}, \text{ and}$$

$$H = \begin{bmatrix} 2 & -2 \\ -2 & 4 \end{bmatrix}.$$

Iteration 1.

$x_1 = [\,0 \quad 0\,]^t, \ W_1 = I_1 = \{3, 4\}.$

$QP(x_1)$:

$$\text{minimize} \quad -2d_1 - 6d_2 + d_1^2 - 2d_1d_2 + 2d_2^2$$

$$\text{subject to} \quad d_1 = 0, \, d_2 = 0.$$

$d_1 = [\,0 \quad 0\,]^t$. KKT system for $QP(x_1)$ at d_1 gives $v_3 = -2$ and $v_4 = -6$, hence we need to drop constraint 4 from the working set.

$W_2 = I_2 = \{3\}$, $x_2 = x_1 = [\,0 \quad 0]^t$.

Iteration 2.

$x_2 = [\,0 \quad 0]^t$, $W_2 = I_2 = \{3\}$.

$QP(x_2)$:

$$\text{minimize} \quad -2d_1 - 6d_2 + d_1^2 - 2d_1d_2 + 2d_2^2$$

$$\text{subject to} \quad d_1 = 0.$$

$d_2 = [\,0 \quad 3/2\,]^t$. Vector $x_2 + d_2$ violates constraints 1 and 2, therefore, we need to determine the step length α_2.

For constraint 1: $A_1^t d_2 = 2$ and $b_1 - A_1^t x_2 = 2$

For constraint 2: $A_2^t d_2 = 3$ and $b_2 - A_2^t x_2 = 2$

Therefore, $\alpha_2 = \min(2/2, 2/3\} = 2/3$, and $q = 2$.

$W_3 = I_3 = \{\,2, 3\}$, and $x_3 = x_2 + \alpha_2 d_2 = [\,0 \quad 1\,]^t$.

Iteration 3.

$x_3 = [\,0 \quad 1]^t$, $W_3 = I_3 = \{\,2, 3\,\}$.

$QP(x_3)$:

$$\text{minimize} \quad -4d_1 - 2d_2 + d_1^2 - 2d_1d_2 + 2d_2^2$$

$$\text{subject to} \quad -d_1 + 2d_2 = 0$$

$$d_1 = 0.$$

$d_3 = [\,0 \quad 0\,]^t$. KKT system for $QP(x_3)$ at d_3 gives $v_2 = 1$ and $v_3 = -5$, hence we need to drop constraint 3 from the working set.

$W_4 = I_4 = \{2\}$, $x_4 = x_3 = [\,0 \quad 1\,]^t$.

Iteration 4.

$x_4 = [\, 0 \quad 1]^t$, $W_4 = I_4 = \{2\}$.

$QP(x_4)$:

$$\text{minimize} \quad -4d_1 - 2d_2 + d_1^2 - 2d_1d_2 + 2d_2^2$$

$$\text{subject to} \quad -d_1 + 2d_2 = 0.$$

$d_4 = [\, 5 \quad 5/2 \,]^t$. Vector $x_2 + d_2$ violates constraint 1 only, therefore,

$$\alpha_4 = \frac{b_1 - A_1^t x_4}{A_1^t d_4} = \frac{1}{7.5} = \frac{2}{15},$$

and $q = 1$.

$W_5 = I_5 = \{\, 1, 2 \,\}$, and $x_5 = x_4 + \alpha_4 d_4 = [\, 2/3 \quad 4/3 \,]^t$.

Iteration 5.

$x_5 = [\, 2/3 \quad 4/3]^t$, $W_5 = I_5 = \{\, 1, 2 \,\}$.

$QP(x_5)$:

$$\text{minimize} \quad -\frac{10}{3}d_1 - 2d_2 + d_1^2 - 2d_1d_2 + 2d_2^2$$

$$\text{subject to} \quad d_1 + d_2 = 0$$

$$-d_1 + 2d_2 = 0.$$

$d_5 = [\, 0 \quad 0 \,]^t$. KKT system for $QP(x_5)$ at d_5 gives $v_1 = 25/9$ and $v_2 = -4/9$, hence we need to drop constraint 2 from the working set.

$W_6 = I_6 = \{1\}$, $x_6 = x_5 = [\, 2/3 \quad 4/3 \,]^t$.

Iteration 6.

$x_6 = [\, 2/3 \quad 4/3]^t$, $W_6 = I_6 = \{\, 1 \,\}$.

$QP(x_6)$:

$$\text{minimize} \quad -\frac{10}{3}d_1 - 2d_2 + d_1^2 - 2d_1d_2 + 2d_2^2$$

$$\text{subject to} \quad d_1 + d_2 = 0.$$

$d_6 = [\, 2/15 \quad -2/15 \,]^t$. Vector $x_6 + d_6 = [\, 0.8 \quad 1.2 \,]^t$ meets all constraints, hence is feasible to the problem. Take $x_7 = [\, 0.8 \quad 1.2 \,]^t$, $W_7 = I_7 = \{1\}$.

Iteration 7.

$x_7 = [\, 0.8 \quad 1.2 \,]^t$, $W_7 = I_7 = \{\, 1\, \}$.

$QP(x_7)$:

$$\text{minimize} \quad -2.8d_1 - 2.8d_2 + d_1^2 - 2d_1d_2 + 2d_2^2$$

$$\text{subject to} \quad d_1 + d_2 = 0.$$

$d_7 = [\, 0 \quad 0 \,]^t$. KKT system for $QP(x_7)$ at d_7 gives $v_1 = 2.8$. Stop with $x = [\, 0.8 \quad 1.2 \,]^t$ as an optimal solution to the problem.

11.23. Matrix H is positive definite, therefore, $f(x) = \frac{1}{2}x^t H x + c^t x$ is convex. Also, it is differentiable. This implies that $f(x)$ is unbounded below in R^n if and only if no vector x exists for which $\nabla f(x) = 0$. Since $\nabla f(x) = Hx + c$, the proof is completed. $\qquad\qquad\square$

11.31. Substitute expressions for Δ_j given in Exercise 11.29 to obtain the following representation of x in the δ-form:

$$x = \mu_1 + \sum_{j=1}^{k-1}(\mu_{j+1} - \mu_j)\delta_j = \mu_1 + \sum_{j=2}^{k-1}\mu_j\delta_{j-1} + \mu_k\delta_{k-1} - \mu_1\delta_1 - \sum_{j=2}^{k-1}\mu_j\delta_j =$$

$$= \mu_1(1-\delta_1) + \sum_{j=2}^{k-1}\mu_j(\delta_{j-1} - \delta_j) + \mu_k\delta_{k-1}.$$

Therefore, the equations for x in the λ-form and δ-form are equivalent if λ_j, $j = 1, \ldots, k$, is as given in this exercise. Next, define a kxk matrix $T = [\, t_{ij}\,]$, where $t_{ii} = 1$, $t_{i+1} = -1$, and $t_{ij} = 0$ for all remaining (i,j)s. Then, $\lambda = T\delta$. Matrix T is upper triangular and invertible. Since $\delta_0 = 1$, $0 \le \delta_j \le 1$ for $j = 1, \ldots, k-1$, and if $\delta_i = 0$ then $\delta_j = 0$ for all $j > i$, all entries of vector λ as computed from $\lambda = T\delta$ are in the interval [0, 1]. Moreover, $1^t\lambda = 1^t T\delta = \delta_0 = 1$.

Also, since $\delta = T^{-1}\lambda$, where T^{-1} is an upper triangular matrix whose diagonal entries and all entries above it are equal to 1, we obtain $\delta_0 = 1$ and $0 \le \delta_j \le 1$ for $j = 1, \ldots, k-1$ if only $\lambda_j \ge 0$ for $j = 1, \ldots, k$ and $\sum_{j=1}^{k}\lambda_j = 1$.

What remains to show is that the two nonlinear requirements are also equivalent.

Consider the requirement "$\lambda_p \lambda_q = 0$ if μ_p and μ_q are not adjacent ", and suppose that for some $p \in \{1, ..., k\text{-}1\}$ we have $\lambda_p > 0$ and $\lambda_{p+1} > 0$. Then $\lambda_j = 0$ for all the remaining j. From the relationship between λ and δ we then obtain

$$\delta_j = 1 \text{ for } j = 0, 1, ..., p-1$$

$$\delta_p = 1 - \lambda_p = \lambda_{p+1}, \text{ and}$$

$$\delta_{p+1} = \delta_p - \lambda_{p+1} = 0$$

$$\delta_{p+r} = \delta_{p+r-1} - \lambda_{p+r} = 0 \quad \text{for r} = 2, ..., \text{k-p}.$$

Thus the requirement "$\delta_i > 0$ implies that $\delta_j = 1$ for j<i" is met.

Also, if $\lambda_p = 1$ for some $p \in \{1, ..., k\}$ and $\lambda_j = 0$ for all $j \neq p$, then $\delta_j = 1$ for $j \leq p$, and $\delta_j = 0$ for $j > p$.

It can be shown in a similar way that if δ_j, $j = 0, 1, ..., k-1$ satisfy the constraint "$\delta_i > 0$ implies that $\delta_j = 1$ for $j < i$" , then λ_j, $j = 1, ..., k$ are such that "$\lambda_p \lambda_q = 0$ if μ_p and μ_q are not adjacent ". Therefore, the two requirements are equivalent. This completes the proof of the equivalence of the two approximation forms. $\square$

11.34. In case of linear fractional programs, if the feasible region is not bounded, an optimal solution may not exit. This does not necessary mean that the objective function (to be minimized) is unbounded below. As opposed to linear programs we may be faced with cases, when the objective function is bounded but does not attain its lower bound on the feasible region.

Suppose that $q^t x + \beta > 0$ for all feasible solutions x. Let the direction vector d_N given in the exercise be a descent direction of f(x) at x_0 , and let $x_0 + \lambda d_N$ be a feasible solution for all $\lambda \geq 0$, which necessarily yields $q_j \geq 0$. Then $f(x_0 + \lambda d_N) = \dfrac{p^t x_0 + \alpha + \lambda p_j}{q^t x_0 + \beta + \lambda q_j}$, and as $\lambda \to \infty$, the value of $f(x_0 + \lambda d_N)$ goes to $\dfrac{p_j}{q_j}$ if $q_j > 0$, and to $-\infty$ if $q_j = 0$. (For the latter case notice that $p_j < 0$ since $\nabla f(x_0)^t d_N < 0$.)

11.37. a. For any λ_1 and λ_2, and for any $\alpha \in [0, 1]$ we have

$$\theta(\alpha\lambda_1 + (1-\alpha)\lambda_2) = f[x + (\alpha\lambda_1 + (1-\alpha)\lambda_2)d] = f[\alpha x + (1-\alpha)x + (\alpha\lambda_1 + (1-\alpha)\lambda_2)d]$$

$$= f[\alpha(x+\lambda_1 d) + (1-\alpha)(x+\lambda_2 d)] \leq \text{minimum}\{f(x+\lambda_1 d), f(x+\lambda_2 d)\} = \text{minimum}\{\theta(\lambda_1), \theta(\lambda_2).$$

Here, the inequality follows from the assumed quasiconcavity of function f(x). The foregoing

derivation shows that function $\theta(\lambda)$ is also quasiconcave.

b. From Theorem 3.5.3 we can conclude that minimum of function $f(x+\lambda d)$ over an

interval [0, a] must occur at one of the two endpoints. However, at $\lambda = 0$ we have $\theta'(0) = $

$\nabla f(x)^t d < 0$, therefore, the minimum value must occur for $\lambda = a$.

c. Conclusion follows directly from part a. In case of the convex simplex method the line search

reduces to evaluating λ_{max}, and next setting λ_k equal to λ_{max}.

11.41. Substitute $f_2(x) = x_0$ to obtain an equivalent problem:

$$\text{minimize} \quad f_1(x) + x_0^a f_3(x)$$

$$\text{subject to} \quad x_0 = f_2(x).$$

However, since functions $f_2(x)$ and $f_3(x)$ take on positive values, and the objective function is to

minimized, we can replace the equality constraint with the inequality $x_0 \geq f_2(x)$. (For any

optimal solution to this problem, the constraint will be satisfied as equation.) Furthermore, since

$f_2(x)$ is positive for any positive x, so is x_0. This allows us to rewrite the problem as minimize

$\{f_1(x) + x_0^a f_3(x): x_0^{-1}f_2(x) \leq 1, x > 0\}$. Finally, note that if a function h(x) is a posynomial in

$x_1, ..., x_n$, and $x_0 > 0$, then for any real a, $x_0^a h(x)$ is a posynomial in $x_0, x_1, ..., x_n$. Also, a sum

of posynomials is a posynomial. Therefore, the problem:

$$\text{minimize} \{f_1(x) + x_0^a f_3(x): x_0^{-1}f_2(x) \leq 1, x > 0\}$$

is in the form of the standard posynomial geometric program.

In the computational example we have:

$J_0 = \{1, 2\}, J_1 = \{3, 4\}, M = 4$ and $n = 3$ (thus $DD = 0$), $\alpha_1 = \alpha_2 = 1, \alpha_3 = 0.8, \alpha_4 = 0.4$

$a_1^t = [\, 0 \quad -1/2 \quad 1/8 \,]$, $\quad a_2^t = [\, 1/2 \quad 1/4 \quad -1/2 \,]$, $\quad a_3^t = [\, -1 \quad 1/2 \quad 2/3 \,]$, and

$a_4^t = [-1 \quad 1/3 \quad 1\,]$.

Step 1. Solve the dual problem.

Since DD = 0, the dual problem has a unique feasible solution. To find it we need to solve the following system for δ_i, i = 1, ..., 4, and u:

$$
\begin{array}{rcccccccl}
 & \frac{1}{2}\delta_2 & - & \delta_3 & - & \delta_4 & & = & 0 \\
-\frac{1}{2}\delta_1 & +\frac{1}{4}\delta_2 & + & \frac{1}{2}\delta_3 & + & \frac{1}{3}\delta_4 & & = & 0 \\
\frac{1}{8}\delta_1 & -\frac{1}{2}\delta_2 & + & \frac{2}{3}\delta_3 & + & \delta_4 & & = & 0 \\
\delta_1 & +\ \delta_2 & & & & & & = & 1 \\
 & & & \delta_3 & + & \delta_4 & -u & = & 0.
\end{array}
$$

The unique solution to this system, and therefore the unique optimal solution to the dual problem, is $\delta_1^* = 20/41$, $\delta_2^* = 21/41$, $\delta_3^* = 15/82$, $\delta_4^* = 3/41$, $u^* = 21/82$. The optimal value of the objective function computed from equation (11.62a) is $\nu^* = 0.738200485$.

Step 2. Compute optimal values of y_i, i = 1, 2, 3.

Values of y_i, i = 1, 2, 3 can now be computed from equations (11. 71a) and (11.71b). In this case the system of equations that we need to solve is as follows:

$$
\begin{array}{rcrcrcr}
 & -\frac{1}{2}y_2 & +\frac{1}{8}y_3 & = & 0.20360691 \\
\frac{1}{2}y_1 & +\frac{1}{4}y_2 & -\frac{1}{2}y_3 & = & 0.069150856 \\
-y_1 & +\frac{1}{2}y_2 & +\frac{2}{3}y_3 & = & -0.113328685 \\
-y_1 & +\frac{1}{3}y_2 & +\ y_3 & = & -0.336472236.
\end{array}
$$

One can notice that the last equation is a linear combination of the remaining three equations, hence it is redundant. The system yields the following solution:

$y_1^* = -0.531128891$, $y_2^* = -0.237804609$, and $y_3^* = -0.788332908$.

Step 3. Compute optimal values of x_0, x_1, and x_2.

From transformation (11.51) we obtain $y_1^* = \ln(x_0^*)$, $y_2^* = \ln(x_1^*)$, and $y_3^* = \ln(x_2^*)$, hence

$x_0^* = 0.587940873$, $x_1^* = 0.788356713$, and $x_2^* = 0.454602027$.

11.42. Readily. the problems

$$\text{minimize} \quad f_1(x) + \frac{f_2(x)}{[f_3(x) - f_4(x)]^a}$$

and

$$\text{minimize} \quad f_1(x) + f_2(x)x_0^{-a}$$

$$\text{subject to} \quad x_0 + f_4(x) \le f_3(x)$$

are equivalent. Also note that $f_3(x)$ is positive-valued, hence the constraint in the latter problem can be rewritten as $\frac{x_0}{f_3(x)} + \frac{f_4(x)}{f_3(x)} \le 1$. It remains to show that the objective function as well as the expression on the left-hand side of the foregoing inequality are posynomials. Readily, if $f_1(x)$ and $f_2(x)$ are posynomials in $x_1, ..., x_n$, then $f_1(x) + f_2(x)x_0^{-a}$ is a posynomial in $x_0, x_1,$ ..., x_n. By assumption, $f_3(x)$ is a single-term posynomial, hence, let $f_3(x) = \alpha \prod_{j=1}^{n} x_j^{a_j}$.

Then $\frac{x_0}{f_3(x)} = \frac{1}{\alpha} \prod_{j=0}^{n} x_j^{\bar{a}_j}$, where $\bar{a}_j = -a_j$ for $j = 1, ..., n$, and $\bar{a}_0 = 1$. This shows that $\frac{x_0}{f_3(x)}$ is a posynomial. Similarly, let $f_4(x) = \sum_{k \in J_4} \alpha_k \prod_{j=1}^{n} x_j^{a_{kj}}$. Then $\frac{f_4(x)}{f_3(x)} = \sum_{k \in J_4} \bar{\alpha}_k \prod_{j=1}^{n} x_j^{\bar{a}_{kj}}$, where for each $k \in J_4$, $\bar{\alpha}_k = \alpha_k / \alpha$, and $\bar{a}_{kj} = a_{kj} - a_j$. This shows that the constraint function is also a posynomial, and thus completes the proof. $\qquad\square$

11.43. Let x^* solve the problem to minimize $f_1(x) - f_2(x)$. By assumption, $f_2(x^*) - f_1(x^*) > 0$. Therefore, (x_0^*, x^*) solves the following problem: maximize $\{x_0 : x_0 \le f_2(x) - f_1(x)\}$. Furthermore, since $f_2(x)$ is a positive valued function, and maximization of x_0 is equivalent here minimization of its reciprocal, we obtain the following equivalent optimization problem:

minimize $\{x_0^{-1} : \frac{x_0}{f_2(x)} + \frac{f_1(x)}{f_2(x)} \le 1\}$. Finally let us note that by same arguments as those in answer to Exercise 11.42, it can be easily shown that both the objective function and the left-hand side function are posynomials. $\qquad\square$